Religion without Redemption

Decolonial Studies, Postcolonial Horizons

Series editors:
Ramón Grosfoguel (University of California at Berkeley)
Barnor Hesse (Northwestern University)
S. Sayyid (University of Leeds)

Since the end of the Cold War, unresolved conjunctures and crises of race, ethnicity, religion, diversity, diaspora, globalisation, the West and the non-West, have radically projected the meaning of the political and the cultural beyond the traditional verities of left and right. Throughout this period, Western developments in 'international relations' have become increasingly defined as corollaries to national 'race relations' across both the European Union and the United States, where the re-formation of Western imperial discourses and practices has been given particular impetus by the 'war against terror'. At the same time, hegemonic Western continuities of racial profiling and colonial innovations have attested to the incomplete and interrupted institution of the postcolonial era. Today we are witnessing renewed critiques of these postcolonial horizons at the threshold of attempts to inaugurate the political and cultural forms that decolonisation now needs to take within and between the West and the 'non-West'. This series explores and discusses radical ideas that open up and advance understandings of these politically multicultural issues and theoretically interdisciplinary questions.

Also available:

Rewriting Exodus
American Futures from Du Bois to Obama
Anna Hartnell

The Dutch Atlantic
Slavery, Abolition and Emancipation
Kwame Nimako and Glenn Willemsen

Islam and the Political
Theory, Governance and International Relations
Amr G.E. Sabet

The Politics of Islamophobia
Race, Power and Fantasy
David Tyrer

Religion without Redemption

Social Contradictions and Awakened Dreams in Latin America

Luis Martínez Andrade

Translated by Antonio Carmona Báez
Foreword by Michael Löwy

PlutoPress
www.plutobooks.com

First published in Spanish as *Religión sin redención. Contradicciones sociales y sueños despiertos en América Latina*, © Taberna Libraria Editores, second edition, 2012.

First English-language edition published 2015 by Pluto Press
345 Archway Road, London N6 5AA

www.plutobooks.com

La presente publicación fue realizada con el estímulo del Programa de Apoyo a la Traducción (PROTRAD), dependiente de las instituciones culturales de México convocantes.
This publication was made possible with the help of the Translation Support Programme (PROTRAD), which has been established by a number of Mexican cultural institutions.

British Library Cataloguing in Publication Data
A catalogue record for this book is available from the British Library

ISBN   978 0 7453 3574 2   Hardback
ISBN   978 0 7453 3572 8   Paperback
ISBN   978 1 7837 1293 9   PDF eBook
ISBN   978 1 7837 1295 3   Kindle eBook
ISBN   978 1 7837 1294 6   EPUB eBook

This book is printed on paper suitable for recycling and made from fully managed and sustained forest sources. Logging, pulping and manufacturing processes are expected to conform to the environmental standards of the country of origin.

10   9   8   7   6   5   4   3   2   1

Typeset by Stanford DTP Services, Northampton, England
Text design by Melanie Patrick
Simultaneously printed by CPI Antony Rowe, Chippenham, UK
and Edwards Bros in the United States of America

In memory of Frantz Fanon

Marx lays bare the causal connection between economy and culture. For us, what matters is the thread of expression. It is not the economic origins of culture that will be presented, but the expression of the economy in its culture.

Walter Benjamin

Contents

Foreword

Luis Martínez Andrade is a brilliant young Mexican scholar, whose writings, published in Spanish, Portuguese, Polish, English and French, are beginning to attract world-wide attention. His essay on shopping malls, included in this book, received first prize for the 2009 international competition Thinking Against the Current, organised by the Cuban Book Institute. This volume is a collection of essays, on very different topics; however, in spite of the diversity, it holds remarkable unity and coherence, given by his theoretical/political approach: a critical Marxist viewpoint, from an emancipatory – that is, anti-capitalist – Latin American perspective. The multiplicity of his intellectual sources in radical theory, both European and Latin American, is impressive: Walter Benjamin and the Frankfurt School, Antonio Gramsci and Ernst Bloch, world-system analysis (Immanuel Wallerstein), philosophy of liberation (Enrique Dussel), decoloniality (Anibal Quijano), liberation theology (Leonardo Boff), and other renowned writers such as Walter Mignolo, Gianni Vattimo, Slavoj Žižek.

Martínez Andrade uses this rich body of cultural tools in order to develop his own thinking. This applies also to the numerous references to my writings: they only appear if useful to the assertion of his own arguments. His writings are not idle academic exercises, but inspired, as he tells us in his prologue, by *rage* – the 'noble rage' (*digna rabia*) proudly asserted by the Mexican Zapatistas – and *hope*: rage against the injustice of the system, and hope in a radical alternative.

One of the most original aspects of the book is the combination of the classical Marxist analysis of imperialism with the arguments of decolonial thinking. Thanks to his roots in Mexican indigenous culture and collective memory, Martínez Andrade clearly understands the real meaning of the so-called 'Discovery of the Americas': a violent and brutal enterprise of colonial conquest, which until today shapes the behaviour of the ruling oligarchy in the continent. The system of domination in Latin America is still based on the *coloniality of power* (Anibal Quijano), that is, the racist segregation and ruthless exploitation, both by the imperialist/colonial powers and the local ruling classes, of the Indigenous, Black and *mestizo* masses that constitute the majority of the population. Moreover, the processes of knowledge and the social sciences are deeply shaped by epistemological paradigms which produce and reproduce dependency and colonial domination.

Max Weber, in his celebrated lecture on 'Science as vocation' (2004 [1919]) spoke of the conflict between irreducibly antagonistic systems of values as a 'War of Gods' (*Kampf der Götter*). A similar sort of conflict is the red thread running through the essays of Martínez Andrade's book: the war between the God of Commodity, the new Golden Calf, and the God of the Poor, celebrated by liberation theology.

As Ernst Bloch and Walter Benjamin, as well as the Latin American theologists, had grasped, capitalism functions as a sort of religion. Its idols – the Market, Money, Capital, the Foreign Debt and Competition – are ruthless, and require human sacrifices: the lives of the poor. Shopping malls are temples for the Commodity-cult and the fanatical adoration of the Holy Brands.

The opposite side in this War of Gods is religion as *Spirit of Utopia*, or as the *Principle of Hope* (Ernst Bloch), which has its roots in the biblical prophets and the first Christian communities, and took a new subversive form during the sixteenth-century Peasant War (Friedrich Engels) under the leadership of the revolutionary theologian Thomas Müntzer. Latin American liberation theology – represented by Leonardo Boff, Frei Betto, Rubén Dri, Jung Mo Sung, Hugo Assmann and many others – is the inheritor of this radical tradition; its intransigent opposition to the capitalist religion, particularly in its deadliest form, neoliberalism, and its unconditional commitment to the self-emancipation of the poor contributed powerfully to the upsurge of social movements and revolutionary struggles, and changed the history of Latin America.

Through its unique synthesis of theology and revolution, heterodox Marxism and leftist postcolonialism, anti-capitalist social science and anti-colonial epistemology, philosophy and (critique of) political economy, ecology and socialism, Martínez Andrade's collection of essays is a fascinating contribution to the renewal of Critical Theory at the beginning of the twenty-first century. His radical Latin American perspective is certainly one of the reasons for the originality and forcefulness of his insights.

Michael Löwy
Paris, 5 August 2014

Prologue

The essays that the reader now holds in her/his hands have been written at different latitudes but all hold the same origin. On the one hand, they were born out of rage and, on the other, out of hope. Rage due to the dire situation with which most of humanity is confronted and the terrible level of exploitation that brings both human life and the entire planet to the edge of destruction. This should not be interpreted as some naïve irritation, commonly found among those 'warm souls' who, when watching children die of hunger, cry for the suffering of the most vulnerable. No. Our abhorrence stems from something else. It is a hate with class. It is a noble rage.

It is through the emancipatory social movements – as another expression of class – that we find the possibility of rupture with history's continuum. The hope for that-which-is-not-yet obliges us to move, and gives meaning to the struggles of liberation and the questions facing the non-truths of discourses.

Strange as it may seem, the brief essays compiled in this book are products of long journeys, many debates and various learning experiences. This does not mean that they are complete. To the contrary. They are suggestions and tracks that I would like to share with the purpose of advancing on the path of hope, as 'we walk while asking and listening'. Some parts have already been presented in colloquiums, others published in academic journals. Nevertheless, the articles have been modified and re-elaborated in order to attain better comprehension.

The book is divided into two parts. The first, 'Entelechies and Cathedrals', serves as a critical interpretation of the relation between modern hegemony and the dynamic of capital. Hence, in this section we are moved to look critically at appearances because, if we want to contribute to the emancipation of humanity, we must then question fetishised truths. In this sense, a critique of and reference to the hegemonic form – that is, the capitalist system as a specific social relation and its diverse expressions – is essential. The religious character of capitalism will be demonstrated so that, in this way, we can find its specific manifestations in Latin America.

The second half, 'Utopia and Liberation' responds to our interest in understanding the important proposals coming out of our continent. The subversive core of the utopic function – expressed through liberation theology, should be reflected upon as a revolutionary project. That project has gone under many different names: trans-modernity, bio-civilisation and eco-socialism, among others. Nevertheless, the labels do not produce irreconcilable disagreements, given that for all these projects the priority lies in the liberation of humanity and of Earth. Without doubt, the contributions of Critical Theory and the philosophy of liberation play an important role in the development of these reflections, as they allow us to recognise the constant movement and immanent contradictions of reality and the geopolitics of the loci of enunciations, the emancipatory nucleus of liberating *ratio* and the ethnic-racial mechanisms of domination and exploitation.

Here, I would like to acknowledge my admiration for the social movements and people who have inspired many of the questions I raise here. To them, I am eternally indebted. I am especially thankful for that insubordinate Marxist, Michael Löwy, a true expression of the organic intellectual from whom I have learned much throughout these years.

Special thanks to Fernando Matamoros, David Cabajal López, Juan Carlos Martínez Andrade, Alí Calderon and especially to Marianna Musial, who have been accomplices in this intellectual enterprise. To this end, I am grateful for the work done by Antonio Carmona Báez on this English-language translation. I would also like to thank the team at *Praktyka Teoretyczna* journal in Poland and their editor Krystian Szadkowski. Finally, thanks to Sophie Richmond for her rigorous and elegant help with corrections. For all the errors and weaknesses found in this book, *mea culpa, mea culpa, mea maxima culpa.*

Part One

Entelechies and Cathedrals

1

Civilising Paradigms
and Colonial Atavisms:
Power and Social Sciences

The sixteenth century shaped not only the identity of what would later become Latin America but also laid the basis for the emergence of the capitalist world-system (Wallerstein, 1999), the emergence of the coloniality of power (Quijano , 2000) and the advent of modernity (Dussel, 1994). These events profoundly influenced the endogenous and exogenous dynamics of different societies and human groups. In the late fifteenth century, and at the dawn of the sixteenth century, such transcendental phenomena were generated in everyday life around the world (*Lebenswelt*). The year 1492 represents a foundational moment in the collective imaginary of modern Western subjectivity, as it involved not only the concealment of the Other but also the pragmatic and specific denial of what is considered to be different (Dussel, 1994). Capitalism, modernity and coloniality arise simultaneously. The analysis – diachronic or synchronic – of the socio-historical form[1] of one of these phenomena should not unravel the study of the civilisation triad. Coloniality, modernity and capitalism are intertwined phenomena that have shaped different relations of domination; various control mechanisms and multiple patterns of exploitation in favour of elite interests.

Throughout Latin American history, the phenomenon of colonialism has shown similar characteristics (domination, racism, humiliation, imposition and violence) with different paradigmatic nuances (Hispanisation, Eurocentrism, the American Way of Life). In this sense, we could say that colonialism is a geopolitically determined socio-historical form. The process of coloniality disrupts all levels of social reality, that is, its teleological dynamics can be seen in the field of culture, epistemology, politics, religion, education, etc.[2] Therefore, the phenomenon of colonialism is embedded in various projects undertaken by the hegemonic dominant classes. The commodification of social life and the fetishisation of power need to be studied from a critical, negative outlook, since reality must be conceived as perpetual motion, constant disruptions and continuous explosions. Understanding (*Verstehen*) and explaining (*Erklären*)[3] society implies recognising its conflicting and contradictory nature.

From the epistemic colonial difference[4] – which is where we stand – we will analyse critically the horizons of civilising paradigms in Latin America. It is necessary to insist, however, first, that this work focuses on the process of neo-colonialism in Latin America. In this sense, we will not develop a historiographical argument but a socio-historical deconstruction of the colonial/modern/capitalist form. Second, it is evident that social relations are not homogeneous, much less static. We can, however, identify some common features (domination, resistance, struggle, conflict, etc.) that characterise Latin American societies[5] as colonised societies. Finally, we argue that it is not reality that must conform to the theories, concepts or categories. On the contrary, the analytical tools used to perform critical analysis of the specific social form need to be appropriate.

Ego Conquiro *and Modern Subjectivity*

The year 1492 is significant in the formation of modern Western subjectivity since it marks the founding moment for what would evolve into its concrete symbolic conscience. On 6 January of that year, Boabdil (Muhammad XII) surrendered in Granada. On 15 February, Torquemada announced his project to commence the expulsion of the Jews from the peninsula. On 17 April, there was the signing of the Santa Fe Accords and on 31 July, the Jews began to leave Castile and Aragon by decree. On 12 October of that same year, there was an 'encounter' between two worlds that had previously been disconnected commercially and ideologically. It was against this backdrop, and from the socio-political and cultural upheaval of the Iberian world, that there arose myths of an inquisatorial, prophetic and apocalyptic modernity.

The 'discovery' of America is a myth constructed by a European narrative. The legend of the three ships,[6] which sailed from the Canary Islands on 8 September 1492 led by one Genovese man, serves as an ideological substratum of a Western historiographical narrative. To affirm

ERRATA

This publication was made possible with the support of Programa de Apoyo a la Traducción (PROTRAD), dependent on Mexican cultural institutions.

Esta publicación fue realizada con el estímulo del Programa de Apoyo a la Traducción (PROTRAD) dependiente de instituciones culturales mexicanas.

that Europeans were the first to reach the 'New World' only helps to consolidate what has been termed 'one unique view of history' (Benjamin, 1969). By this, with Walter Benjamin (2001), we are referring to an idea that stands alone in history, isolated from events unfolding around it; an event that is a representation of the past constructed by the dominant groups and classes of the time. The 'discovery' of America by Europeans was little more than recognition of cartographies that had already been drawn up. Enrique Dussel (1994) noted that the world map of Heinrich Hammer (also known as Henricus Martellus) had similarly revealed the presence of our continent as early as 1489.

Pomeranz (2004), Mignolo (2003) and Dussel (2004) have brought to the fore a number of political, economic and social factors that shaped Columbus' adventure. It is worthy of note that, at the time, the *mare nostrum* was not known as the commercial 'centre' of the 'inter-regional market'; at the time, the leading centre of trade was located between the East China Sea and the Bay of Bengal. Importantly, Europe needed China and, as Walter Mignolo (2001: 22) pointed out: 'the Atlantic route emerges as a possibility following the Ottoman blockade of the route from China and India'. The role of China is critical to understanding Columbus and the formation of the world-system. Menzies (2003) and Dussel (2004) discuss how, in the first half of the fifteenth century, the Chinese had circumnavigated the planet. However, China abandoned its maritime domain in 1424 following a decision taken by the Ming emperors (1368–1644). This undoubtedly led to a vacuum of power and the growth of commercial shipping in the 'market-world', a fact that later benefited Europe in its endeavours. The measure taken by the empire excluded any possibility of China monopolising the Atlantic.

China was the 'centre' of the Euro-Afro-Asian market, and its technological, economic and military supremacy ensured that it was exempt from the need to reach across the sea; unlike the case in Europe.[7] It was a simple commercial imperative for the Europeans to find a path to the East and, by relentlessly pursuing trade routes, European sailors inevitably came across a different continent, making the Atlantic theirs.

Walter Mignolo (2001) argues that the emergence of the Atlantic circuit in the sixteenth century had, among other things, two main consequences. It connected the trade circuit of Anahuac with that of Tawantinsuyu and, at the same time, connected them to the Western world market. The outcome was thus the genesis of a world-system. For Wallerstein (1999), the world-system was borne out of the sixteenth century with its interconnecting world markets. The transatlantic perspective presented by Wallerstein is crucial to understanding the emergence of capitalism – and its dynamics – on a global scale. Seized by Spain and Portugal, hegemony over the Atlantic bestowed resources (such as labour and metal) upon Europe, contributing to the *rise of the West*. Yet, contrary to Wallerstein (1991), Dussel (2004) argues that hegemony over the Atlantic did not imply the centrality of Europe in the world-system, instead maintaining that it was not until the British Industrial Revolution in the eighteenth century that this would come to fruition.

The emergence of the Atlantic route was fundamental to the origin of the world-system as it synchronised world markets that were previously disconnected. The genesis of the world-system was simultaneously the advent of the first colonial panorama, which involved the subjection of Indigenous forced labour. In a sense, the world-system was built on a geopolitically determined 'racial division of labour' (Quijano, 2001). Hence, we now make reference to a modern/colonial world-system. Enrique Dussel (1993) maintains that modernity is intimately linked to colonisation processes in Latin America and the Caribbean. For him, modernity is not an exclusively intra-European phenomenon[8] and constitutes a relation to an Otherness denied, that of the (*Cemanahuac*) Indigenous world.

Modern subjectivity was established by the Conquest of America, since Europe had no effective self-consciousness of superiority prior to 1492. Europe demonstrated an awareness of the economic, intellectual and political superiority of the Muslim, Chinese and Ottoman worlds. Modern subjectivity is marked by violence that the Spanish imposed upon Indigenous peoples. The statement 'God is in heaven, the King is far away, I am in command', is a significant reflection of the founding moment of the modern Western ego. The *ego conquiro* (I conquer) precedes *ego cogito* (I think) (Dussel, 2013) – by nearly a century (and proposed by Descartes in 1636), therefore making it a 'critical' moment in awareness of Western superiority as it is the first sign of Europe's will for power. The *ratio* as an instrument of domination, exclusion and suppression comprised a new ontology after 1492.

For Enrique Dussel, modernity holds certain ambivalence, with elements constantly in tension. While one is linked to the process of emancipation, that is, escaping the state of human immaturity, the other refers to the justification of an irrational praxis of violence.[9] In this sense, the libertarian core *ratio* is accompanied by a constant drive towards the immolation of a different Otherness. From its birth, modernity perpetuated a constitutive ritual sacrifice to build the modern Western subjectivity. It is a liturgy that has been repeated over the past five centuries and one that has had immeasurable victims. Reason, progress and development stand as the pillars of colonial *logos*, with the messianic figure of modernity concealing the predator's cruel and bloody face.

The crimes carried out by the *ego conquiro* of modern Western subjectivity should not be omitted in one single act of liberating deconstruction, as this would only strengthen the impunity of existing historico-cultural colonial discourses. Epistemic vigilance – to use a term employed by Bourdieu (2002b) – may not, in fact, be separated from memory; that is, beyond the pipe dream of 'axiological neutrality', we must recognise those interests involved in the configuration of social spaces across time.

Coloniality of Power and the World-System

Immanuel Wallerstein coined the term *modern world-system* in order to depict the formation and composition of capitalist dynamics globally. Employing a transatlantic perspective, and influenced naturally by dependency theory, Wallerstein developed original analytic categories which allowed him to understand-explain the logic of capital.

Wallerstein maintains that, from its origins in the sixteenth century, the world-system produced structural inequalities among trading regions, starting with the extraction of resources in the Americas, allowing for the establishment and growth of unequal relations. In this sense, Latin America constituted Europe's first periphery. We should bear in mind, nevertheless, that the centrality of Europe in the world-system does not congeal until the eighteenth century (Dussel, 2004).

For Latin America and the Caribbean, the emergence of the modern world-system marked the advent of the first colonial horizons. Portuguese-Spanish domination created the conditions for what Aníbal Quijano describes as the *coloniality of power*. In fact, world-system and coloniality of power are collaterally synchronic. The pattern of domination between the colonisers and the colonised was organised on the principle of 'race'.[10] The practical consequences of the categorisations were not only the dispossession of peoples from their lands but also the dispossession of identities, that is, Aztecas, Incas, Mayas, Araucanos, Aymaras and so on became Indians. The coloniality of power ran parallel to the establishment of a new cognitive pattern. The evangelisation of Indigenous peoples resulted not only in the penetration of their imaginary ethical-mythical core but also the reconfiguration of their epistemologies.

To this Aníbal Quijano (2000) adds that: 'America, modernity and capitalism were all born on the same day.' This reiterates that the imposition of the first colonial panorama is coeval with the formation of sixteenth-century Spanish America. The emergence of historical capitalism, therefore, cannot be divorced from the colonial spectre of Latin America and the explosions of constellations which imply ruptures of power.

The idea of race, Quijano (1998) tells us, had been formed during the wars of 'Reconquest' on the Iberian peninsula, given that in those wars the Christians of the Counter-Reformation amalgamated in their perception religious differences with those of phenotypes. How else does one explain the requiring of Certificates of Blood Purity, which the victors established for the Muslims and Jews? The concept of race was born with America, modernity and the (modern) world-system, and appears as the centrepiece of social and cultural relations founded upon biological differences.

With the creation of racial classifications came the practices of social domination, control and socio-ethnic exploitation. The fateful conditions of labour and slavery exterminated the Indigenous peoples of the Caribbean[11] almost entirely and undermined considerably the native populations of the continent. For this reason, the Crown of Castile decided to move from slavery to servitude, as its most prized possession – the Indigenous workforce – were in danger of extinction. The Spaniards invented new forms of forced labour, like the *encomienda*, which became a mode of production within capitalism.[12] In fact, 'from this mode a systematic racial division of labour was imposed' (Quijano, 2000: 204).

The racial organisation of labour was being articulated in the dynamics of capital. The rate of Indigenous mortality brought the Europeans to import a workforce through the slave trade.[13] The workforce (of Indigenous and Black populations), objectified in the products that were exported to European markets, and therefore inscribed into world-system logic, did not earn salaries. Nevertheless, it is known that the Spaniards and Portuguese (the dominant races) were the judges of that right, and the racially differentiated social pyramid was born.

The coloniality of power, as a pattern of domination-exploitation, was configured upon a racial organisation of labour. In this sense, starting from the sixteenth century, race/labour founded not only asymmetric but also somatically differentiated social relations.[14] According to Katzew (2004), the depictions of castes are particularly exemplary, as these participate in the construction of racial identities linked to social stratification through visual representation. For Katzew, the paintings of castes suggest a basic principle: White or Spanish blood implied a degree of civilisation, while Black blood expressed backwardness and depravity. It is important to keep these notations in mind, as they are still part-and-parcel of the Latin American imaginary.

The world-system and the coloniality of power are coeval in the formation of modern subjectivity, given that its hegemonic *logos* is mediated by social relations of control, domination and exploitation. The coloniality of power, as a critical concept, considers historic-structural dependency and the specific characteristics of Latin America. The uniqueness of original peoples was violently subjected to Western absolute[15] universality. Throughout this process of identification and classification, Indigenous people never ceased to struggle[16] and resistance to colonialism certainly remained constant. Nevertheless, since the Conquest of the Americas, a new power relationship has been implemented, not only socially but at an epistemic level as well.

Edgardo Lander (2000) points out that it was through the separations or partitioning of reality that Western epistemology came into being. The rupture between subject and object is correlated to the Hellenic-Christian[17] separation between God, man and nature. In this sense, the colonisers-evangelisers shared a knowledge based on the estrangement between the body and soul, implying a subalternisation of knowledge. At the same time, the coloniality of power involved the 'coloniality of knowing'.

The teleological dynamic of the coloniality of power and knowledge gave birth to the coloniality of doing in Latin American and Caribbean society.[18] With the coloniality of doing, we refer to the colonial discursive practices, naturalised above all by the *mestizo* population in a symbolic-cultural context. If race/work/gender (Quijano, 2001) articulate the concept of the coloniality of power, then it is the habitus of the imaginary and double consciousness which configures the 'coloniality of doing'.

The coloniality of doing permits us to distinguish aesthetic, linguistic, symbolic and cultural practices. Undoubtedly, social relations imply struggle, tensions and ruptures. The coloniality of doing, however, recognises the continuities of the structures of domination. The link between culture and power could be revealed through this analytical tool.

Eduard Glissant (1997) uses the term 'imaginary' to refer to the symbolic construction through which a community defines itself. For this Antillean thinker, the word does not connote a mental image, much less a technical form where the imaginary is part of a differentiation structure between the Symbolic and the Real. The imaginary is not only constituted in and through colonial power, rather it is also made by ruptures and responses of communities, groups and classes that the colonial discourse uses in its own description (Mignolo, 2000).

As of the sixteenth century, we witness a struggle of imaginaries (colonisers and the colonised) in constant transformation. The conquerors tried to impose their imaginary through religion, to later inculcate their own values, *Weltanschauung*, culture and morals. It is fundamental to understand that the imaginary, like reality, is not a static, neutral and immobile process; on the contrary it is dynamic and in constant tension.

On the other hand, the concept of double consciousness was formulated by the sociologist W.E.B. Du Bois (1990) to characterise the dilemma of subjectivities forged in the colonial reality; that is to say, amid the processes experienced in the daily lives (*Lebenswelt*) of the subaltern. If Du Bois used this notion to explain the uniqueness of the Afro-American experience, as a subaltern group, then for our part we can incorporate it into the comprehension-explanation of the processes of subjection of the *criollos* or *mestizos* of Latin American and Caribbean societies.

Walter Mignolo (2000) is convinced that the principle of double consciousness characterises the imaginary of the modern colonial world from the margins of the empires. For him, the emergence of the 'Western hemisphere' marked the insertion of the *criollos* of European descent into the colonial imaginary. Mignolo (2000: 68) makes a distinction between the White *criollos* and the Black *criollos*, given that the latter: 'were not the conscious heirs of the colonisers and emigrants, rather, they were the heirs of slavery'. The White *criollo* double consciousness would become concretely distinguished from the *mestizo* double consciousness, given that the racial divide continues to be of the utmost importance in the social relations of the colonial world. The White *criollo* will affirm his difference towards Europe in political and cultural terms, but never when it comes to phenotypes. Frantz Fanon (2004), for one, analysed the processes of subjection experienced by the colonised in the context of racial discrimination. In his work, *The wretched of the earth* (2004: 5), he describes the existential peculiarities of the colonial imaginary, where the somatic aspect is cardinal in the relations which are established, and maintained that: 'The governing race is first and foremost those who come from elsewhere, those who are unlike the original inhabitants, "the Others".' The double consciousness of the *mestizo* would become central to the formation of a colonial *habitus*. The 'coloniality of doing' becomes evident in discursive practices, which imply preferences, tastes and determined antipathies.

The concept of *habitus* becomes essential in the analysis of domination, given that its value lies in exposing the effects of the system on the doing of the social being. While Bourdieu differentiates between the *habitus* of classes, we make the distinction of the colonial *habitus* of classes. Like all concepts, *habitus* should not substantiate itself. On the contrary, it should dialectically exhibit tensions, struggles and intrinsic contradictions in social relations; in this case, colonial relations.

In Latin America and the Caribbean, the *coloniality of doing* is configured by the *imaginary*, the *double consciousness* and *habitus*. Its specificity should be pronounced geopolitically, given that it is a dynamic process, and therefore heterogeneous and explosive. In the different experience of habitus, the coloniality of doing accentuates the symbolic and cultural features of social practices. The analysis of everyday life is transcendental in the research of historical social sciences, and for this reason the concept is indispensable for the studies of cultural and social processes of peripheral societies.

The formation of nation-states in Latin America reinforced the coloniality of doing and of knowing. The articulation of the world-system of the nation-states is linked to the process of social discipline undergone by the Latin American population. The reconfiguration of the coloniality of power, in the nineteenth century, influenced the way in which citizenship has been understood. Generally, it does not suffice to be a male (gender), you also had to be White (race), possess properties and distinguish oneself from Indigenous people.[19] In this sense, Santiago Castro-Gómez recalls three disciplinary practices which contributed to forge the citizenship of the nineteenth century: constitutions, city ordinances and the grammar of language. According to him, writing was made into an instrument of subjection in the invention of negated Otherness. For Castro-Gómez (2000), the shaping of the citizen, as a 'legal subject' is possible only within the framework of disciplinary writing and, in this sense, within the space of legality defined by the constitution. Hence, the juridical-political function of the constitutions was, precisely, to invent citizenship

– to create a field of homogeneous identities that would make viable the modern project of governability.[20]

The consolidation of the nation-state in Latin America was legitimised by the pipedream of an ineluctable journey towards modernity. The 'state of nature' is then transcended and the 'political state' is instituted via geopolitically determined apparatus or institutions. For this reason, political organisation – as with the constitutions – was established within the confines of Western parameters.

The nation-state and its corollary, citizenship, exercised a disciplining of doing upon groups and individuals. The logic of power was transfigured at the dawn of the nineteenth century, demonstrating that the relations of domination, as well as those of resistance, are not static, much less are they homogeneous.

The colonial paradigm was transfigured and moved to northern Europe (England, Germany and France). Such displacement is significant because it implicitly marginalised the role of Spain and Portugal in the narrative of modernity.[21] In this sense, Europe not only established itself as the centre of the world-system but also began to fabricate an ideology that was imposed in the social imaginary.

From the nineteenth century onwards, Latin American societies suffered the influence of the new imperial powers (England, Germany and France), although this did not cause the fall of the Spanish and Portuguese stronghold. While power changed hands, the White *criollo* core preserved their privileges, as evidenced in the ideological debates between liberals and conservatives.

Just as, during the sixteenth century, Indigenous peoples had to convert to Christianity, the nineteenth-century residents had to become citizens. The coloniality of power was consolidated within the state apparatus, the coloniality of knowledge was strengthened with *Lumière* and *Aufklärung* and the coloniality of doing in the urban ordinances and in civil laws. The civilising mission demanded a refinement of autochthonous discursive practices; in this sense, good morality had to replace socialising forms of the vulgar.[22] The train of progress had taken off and no force, neither in Heaven nor on Earth, could step in its path.

If the process of national independence implies a rupture with patterns of colonial domination, the political, economic and cultural liberation of Latin America has never been achieved. The umbilical cord of foreign dependency was never cut. The civilisational paradigm was simply transfigured. England, Germany and France (Dussel, 2013; Wallerstein,

1998) had gained ground in the 'world-system' and therefore became the new headmasters of the political world. Latin America continued to suffer the imperial yoke.[23] The coloniality of knowing became stronger not only with the ideologies of progress but also with the emergence of the social sciences. From Mexico to Argentina, positivism was inculcated through university classes, through the dogmatism of secular science, and thinkers 'copied and pasted' ideas imported from Europe. In this sense, the social sciences became yet another instrument in the service of colonial power.[24]

The first factual moment in the coloniality of doing took place in the sixteenth century. Conquest and evangelisation were the basis of said process. The second moment was forged at the dawn of the nineteenth century. The White *criollo* nucleus of the region monopolised wealth and power. A social pyramid of somatic social difference was established. In this sense, not only did the idea of race play an important role in the recon-figuration of power; rather, it became a determinant in the social structure. The production of Otherness (Black and Indigenous) was articulated in the consolidation of an 'internal coloniality' which benefited *criollos* and *mestizos*.

The formation of nation-states in Latin America reconfigured the pattern of colonial domination and exploitation. The 'coloniality of doing' was transfigured to a framework where the social sciences, on the one hand, legitimised the ideological-cultural domination of the metropolises and, on the other, the idea that the 'State of Law' was the privilege of certain social groups. The Indigenous would continue to occupy a place outside of the ontological and political system.

Eurocentrism and Social Science

In *The philosophical discourse of modernity*, Habermas (1998: 17) maintains: 'The key historical events in establishing the principle of subjectivity are the Reformation, the Enlightenment, and the French Revolution.' In this archaeology of modernity the spatial-temporal sequence of its antecedents are: Italy (fifteenth century), Germany (sixteenth to eighteenth centuries) and France (eighteenth century). Enrique Dussel (1993) calls this perspective a 'Eurocentric view' because its reference points are intra-European and its subsequent development does not need more than Europe itself to explain the process. It is a reductionist, regional and therefore provincial point of view.

For Dussel (1993, 1994, 2004), modernity should be understood in a global context, and therefore Latin America and the Caribbean are fundamental in the constitution of modernity. He also mentions that generally, in this archaeology, Spain and Portugal are excluded from the process. Is the first stage of modernity of the mercantilist world not significant in the formation of the capitalist spirit?

The characterisation of the concept of modernity, from Kant to Touraine, not only excludes Spain and Portugal from the modern imaginary but also omits the importance of China, Latin America and the Caribbean in the making of Europe as the centre of the world-system. The *Aufklärung* or Enlightenment was the first instance of Eurocentrism, producing shifts in narratives that legitimised an ideologically perverse entelechy.

Enrique Dussel (1994) cites multiple examples of how Spain's cultural, political and military capacities surpassed those of other European countries. By 1492, Spain had achieved a unified peninsula, with an apparatus (the Inquisition) for top-down national consensus, with a military force which destroyed Boabdil, and a grammar edited by Antonio de Nebrija entitled the *Art of the Castilian language*, which placed Castilian on the same level as other noble languages like Greek and Latin.

Spain not only opened the first stage of world mercantilism, it also initiated the creation of the Western modern subjectivity. The role of Spain was significant in the advent of the modern European imaginary and the colonial world-system, as its ethical-mythical nucleus – in terms used by Paul Ricoeur – was shaped in relation to a negated Otherness, that of the Indigenous.

In the first Eurocentrism (Kant, Hegel, Weber), as in the second (Habermas, 1998; Touraine, 1999; Lyotard, 2000), the importance of Spain is not recognised, much less that of Latin America, in the process of constituting modernity and capitalism. China, of course, fell behind in the 'dark night' of oriental despotism characterised in the simple image of the 'Asiatic mode of production' (Dussel, 2004).

In *The protestant ethic and the spirit of capitalism*, Max Weber tries to correlate rational action with religious ethos in the formation of capitalism. For him, 'European exceptionalism' is fundamental. He questions the appearance and authorship of cultural phenomena that give universal meaning and value a Western – and only Western – appearance. In going beyond economic determinism, Weber undoubtedly tried to respond, but he got no further than the boundaries of Eurocentrism.

Weber (2004: 362) points out that the emergence of capitalism is intrinsically linked to the Protestant ethos of Western civilisation. We should emphasise his interest in explaining Western exceptionalism when he says: 'But in the modern period there has appeared in the West ... a quite different kind of capitalism, one that has not developed anywhere else on Earth, namely, the rational, capitalist organisation of (formally) free labour.'

The notion 'formally free labour' brings us to the process of secularisation of the world and the rationalisation of life, given that it involves a specific development of rationalisation – in the instrumental sense – tied to a process of mercantilisation and quantification. For this reason, the idea of 'formally free labour' allows for the articulation of the dynamic of modern, Western capitalism.[25]

Weber's proposal merits critical examination that goes beyond the confines of Eurocentrism. We agree with Weber in identifying a particular form of capitalism enshrined in the logics of calculation, accumulation and modern specific rationality. We disagree, however, in his interpretation of the origin of capitalism.

Weber's perspective does not mention the importance of Latin America in the construction of modern capitalism, even though the 'discovery of America' is fundamental to the expansion of capitalism in its 'primitive accumulation' stage. Moreover, like Dussel (2004), we can connect 'Europe's ascent' with the 'discovery of America'.[26] Michael Beaud (2000), for one, argues that according to official sources, 18,000 tons of silver and 200 tons of gold were transferred from the Americas to Spain between 1521 and 1660. Beaud also states that others estimate that it was double this amount. The mines of Potosí and Zacatecas afforded the Europeans an accumulation of monetary riches that were sufficient to secure the 1571 victory over the Turks at the battle of Lepanto. Europe, once isolated in the periphery of the Hindu, Islamic and Chinese worlds, developed by amassing resources from Latin America.

Eduardo Galeano (1997) described the importance of Latin American resources for imperial interests. The robbing, rape and pillage that was done – and is still happening – is correlated to the structural inequalities intrinsic in the colonial/modern world-system. In this way, Dussel (1994) maintains, the equation presented by the Eurocentric narrative changes and now becomes: Renaissance, Conquest of the Americas, Reform, Enlightenment, French Revolution, etc. The spirit of capitalism and modernity is not a quality that is endogenous to the European world, rather it is a historical construction enshrined in different social phenomena. Included in these is also the case of China.

Enrique Dussel (2004) suggests that centrality of Europe can be calculated as lasting no longer than two centuries. Europe leads the modern/colonial world-system at the dawn of the nineteenth century thanks to the Industrial Revolution in Great Britain. If the Industrial Revolution is another watershed in the Western narrative, what is its relation to the Chinese world? Supported by the contributions of André Gunder Frank (1979) and Kenneth Pomeranz (2004), Enrique Dussel (2004) demonstrated the important role China played in the world-system until the seventeenth century. Even Adam Smith considered China to be a country much richer than any European nation and recognised that the differences in prices of basic goods between the continents were great. For example, rice was much cheaper in China than wheat in Europe.

Kenneth Pomeranz offers another interpretation of the origin of industrial capitalism by looking at ecological imbalance. In the Yangtze valley, the purchase and sale of land was much more advanced than England. However, due to a demographic explosion,[27] China experienced an unprecedented famine and ecological crisis.

In the Yangtze valley there was incipient capitalist production that was hindered by deforestation and destructive land use in the countryside. Furthermore, peasants could not participate in industrial production and salaried workers had to be reintegrated into agricultural production. The Chinese empire decided, for demographic and ecological reasons, to change its economic policy because the social situation became unsustainable. In contrast to England, China had no colonies to which it could send its excess population. In this sense, as Pomeranz (2004) suggests, it was not merely a new ethos (that studied by Max Weber) that created Western industrial capitalism but also an ecological imbalance (in China) which has never been systematically accounted for.

Dussel (1994) recommends that thinking in a non-Eurocentric way is to imagine that the Industrial Revolution was made possible by the 'second vacuum',[28] produced by the market dominated by China and India. Within a few decades, machinery and its subsumption in the process of production gave England a comparative advantage over China, India and the Muslim world, Spanish America, Eastern Europe (Poland and the Russian Empire) and Southern Europe (Italy, Spain and Portugal). Dussel (2004) maintains that the Rise of the West can be explained in its relation to the Decline of the East. Therefore, the Industrial Revolution is a product of a global process that includes China. Its advent and development is based on various exogenous factors. The Hegelian notion of development not only contributed to hiding China's significance as an extremely important culture, but also to consolidating the myth of Western superiority and the civilising mission of European culture.

Immanuel Wallerstein (1991) shows that the world-system implies a determined *geo-culture*, that is, ideologies and worldviews (*Weltanschauungen*) that are produced, modified and transformed within the framework of tensions, in some cases under the same precepts (reason, development, progress, etc.) but with different ideological overtones. In this sense, Wallerstein maintains that the nineteenth century not only created determined ideologies (conservatism, Marxism and liberalism) but also the circumstances for the formation of the social sciences. Wallerstein says that the social sciences are Eurocentric in their roots, given that they attempted to resolve the problems of European societies (England, Germany and France), while serving to legitimise the existence of the state and the logic of capital. For him, social science is a product of the world-system and Eurocentrism is constitutive of the geo-culture of the modern world.

The incipient European hegemony over the world-system implied the projection of a geopolitics of knowledge determined by the West. In this *epistemicide*[29] the Western narrative would impose its myths, imaginaries and beliefs through philosophical and discursive entelechies. Eurocentrism is manifested not only at the concrete, material and socio-political level, but also at an ideological and epistemological plane as well.

Nevertheless, it is important to acknowledge that the 'epistemic continuity'[30] of Western knowledge became entwined with the logic of colonial capitalism. We do not deny that, at the heart of scientific discourse, there were certain significant ruptures (Galileo, Copernicus, Kepler, Descartes); rather, what we recognise is the epistemic continuity in the Western gnoseological process.

Boaventura de Sousa Santos (Santos, 2002) argues that the model of rationality that presides over modern science was constituted during the Scientific Revolution of the sixteenth century and was disentangled during the following centuries under the dominance of the natural sciences. The consolidation of the naturalist model (evolutionist paradigm) was fundamental to the subalternisation of two sorts of potentially disturbing and intrusive non-scientific (and therefore irrational) knowledge: that is, common sense and the so-called humanities. Hence, Santos argues that the new scientific rationality that became global is also totalitarian, in the sense that it negates the rational character of other forms of knowledge that do not submit to its epistemological principles and methodological rules. Such *epistemicide* took root in the total separation between nature and humanity, creating the conditions for the promotion of science without conscience.

The scientific knowledge of the nineteenth century was subject to the laws of Newtonian physics (the notion of causality), the rules of mathematics (quantifying reality) and the postulates of biology (progress and evolution). The geopolitics of knowledge (philosophical, historical, sociological, among others), sustained by the evolutionist perspective legitimised the idea of an 'objective knowledge' of ethno-racial superiority.

The consequences of the *Aufklärung* would become evident in the foundations of the social sciences of the nineteenth century. The sociology of Comte, Durkheim, Tönnies, Weber, Spencer, Marx, etc. takes part in an epistemicide (incubated in the sixteenth century) linked to the dynamic of the modern/colonial world-system. The birth – and tragedy – of the social sciences involved the construction of concepts and categories that legitimised Eurocentric discourse. Subordinated to the prescriptions of the natural sciences (quantification, objectification and causality) and tied to the functioning of the world-system, the social sciences created hard truths[31] and epistemic devices that sustain the colonial hegemonic discourse.

Durkheim and his epistemic posture (treat social facts as things) strengthened the development of an organic sociology. Even though Durkheim was critical of Spencer, we should not forget that their epistemic foundations did not differ that much. The sociology of the nineteenth century, Eurocentric as it was, is essentially colonial.

On occasion, the term 'Western' is conceived only as an analytical category overlooking its geographical aspect. However, we would like to look at two related aspects. The first is gnoseological, given that all theoretical, aesthetic and scientific production has concrete, social and geo-historical reference. In this case, the nineteenth-century thinkers were found in the context of a Europe that was growing economically. The centrality of Europe in the world-system and the evolutionist vision marked the authors' perspectives ideologically. The social panorama and the civilising 'myth' influenced the gnoseological process of the founders of the social sciences. The second aspect is historical. Hegel's *Lectures on the philosophy of history*, like Kant's reflections, imposed a consensus

(ideological, syllogistic and epistemic) of the supposed superiority
of the Western world. On the other hand, it is also important to stress
that if the social sciences of the nineteenth century waged a war against
philosophy in order to achieve scientific status, via intellectual parricide,
their discursive inheritance is essentially philosophical. In this sense, the
hegemonic philosophy that sees Man (at least since the Renaissance) as
a symbolic and material universe, has as its discursive reference point a
concrete basis and distinct ontology – that of the White, European and
therefore Western man.

The coloniality of knowledge strengthened the epistemic dependency
of intellectuals, universities and ideological currents in Latin America.
The theories of Hobbes, Locke, Rousseau, Weber, etc. were thought of as
universally valid in the study of humanity.

In his book, *Society, the state and modern philosophy*, Norberto Bobbio
argued that political *ius* naturalism was initiated by Thomas Hobbes in
1647, as for him, this last English thinker broke with the Aristotelian
model which prevailed during his time. For Hobbes, the idea of Man is
expressed in the *homo homini lupus*. For the naturalists, 'civil society' is
not a prolongation, and much less the perfection of the 'natural state'.
Rather it is the substitution of the same. Civil society is antithetical to
the 'natural state'; it is a state that is diametrically opposed to 'the state
in which certain primitive societies are found, be they the savage peoples
of this era as are some of the Indigenous groups of America or the
barbarians of ancient times now civilised' (Bobbio and Bovero, 1994: 71).
This idea is of paramount importance: it expresses a colonial and racial
vision of non-European peoples. Hence we should ask ourselves: What
are the political and epistemological implications of continuing to work
with concepts and categories that supress the peoples of the periphery?
Does the dichotomy used in the natural model update the savage/civilised
Manichaeism? Do these approaches continue to be valid even when the
ideas of progress, modernity and development have lost legitimacy?

During the 1980s, Abdelkebir Khatibi continued Frantz Fanon's
theoretical project and proposed an 'other thinking' that undertook a
double critique – on the one hand, against Western logo-centrism and, on
the other, ethnocentric exceptionalism. In this sense, Khatibi (1983: 54)
maintained that an 'other thinking' should not be totalising and therefore
neither Marxist in the strict sense – think about the carbon copy models
that were developed in the periphery – and much less anti-Marxist in the
rightist sense of the term. Rather, 'other thinking' is found at the limits of

said possibilities, given that if we want to decentre Western knowledge within us, we need to decentre ourselves from said axis. For this reason, 'other thinking' must be plural. That is, open to all the cultures that have peripheral political, social and epistemic liberation at its horizons.

The social and cultural context of the social sciences in Latin America has to some extent determined the production of such original proposals as dependency theory, pedagogy of liberation, social psychology of liberation, participatory action research (PAR) and postcolonial studies of the liberationist sort. It is no coincidence that the social processes of the last decades are resulting in the creation of emancipatory educational projects. In Brazil, for example, there are 2000 self-managed schools at the Landless Workers' Movement (MST) settlements.

We therefore argue that the decolonisation of the historical social sciences requires a break from the universalising tradition of Eurocentric perspectives and the renunciation of colonial epistemic paradigms. The historical social sciences of Latin America should be linked to a project that contributes to the liberation of societies from their colonial inheritance. From this, liberation becomes the ethical, historical, political and epistemic imperative of the historical social sciences in the Third World. The epistemic anthropophagy should propose the radical transformation of the society for the benefit of human beings who are racially and ontologically different from those who invented colonial ideology.

The analytical conceptual atavism of the historic social sciences concretised in ideological antinomies (traditional/modern, natural state/ civilised state, savage societies/modern societies, organic solidarity/ mechanical solidarity, community/society, among many others), should be de-fetishised through a libertarian *ratio* and a decolonising perspective: 500 years of exploitation and ontological negation are also five centuries of gnoseological domination!

Independence and the Coloniality of Doing

Social processes are negotiated by the relations of power. Contradictory dynamics demonstrate the tensions and conflicts that are forged in societal spaces. Domination, struggle and resistance are components of the social fabric. For this reason, analysing domination implies recognising the subaltern strategies of counter-power.

The period of political independence is very complex and significant, given that it not only represents the formation of nation-states (fundamental to the coloniality of power), but also the configuration of the Latin American 'double consciousness' that as a result would bear a reconstitution of the 'coloniality of doing'. In other words, this means the transfiguration of colonial-civilising paradigms in the social, linguistic and cultural practices of a certain population.

Walter Mignolo (2000) analyses the double consciousness of two important figures (Jefferson and Bolívar) in the continental processes of independence. For Mignolo, Jefferson's English tradition and memory differs in certain respects from Bolívar's Hispanic tradition and memory. Nevertheless, both contributed to the idea of a Western hemisphere and the establishment of a *criollo* – Anglo and Hispanic – identity.[32]

Corporeal or somatic capital[33] is transcendental in the development of the Latin American double consciousness, given that it explains *criollo* and *mestizo* doing (*faire y agir*), not only in the processes of independence but also in everyday life. Mignolo mentions that Jefferson and Bolívar shared an ambivalent feeling towards Europe. On the one hand they sought political differentiation; on the other they felt the same in somatic terms. In this sense, *criollo* double consciousness here is not racial but geopolitical in its relation to Europe.

The *criollo* core (descendants from the peninsula), as being different in somatic capital from the Afro-Americans, *mestizos* and Indigenous, feel linked to European discursive practices. Although at given moments they boast and praise the national identity, they cannot hide their disdain for other groups in the racial pyramid of Latin America.

The *mestizo* double consciousness, marked somatically by the mix between European and Indigenous, is ambivalent in the process of colonisation. Heirs of the Andalusian and Lusitanian tradition on the European side, of the pre-Columbian legacy of Amerindian civilisations and the memory of enslaved Africans, the *mestizo* double consciousness wanders through the bifurcated paths of history. It suffers the disregard of the peninsula and the *criollos* for simply being somatically different from them. It experiences Indigenous distrust for being a product of the invader and becomes nothing more than a simple *ladino*.

The *mestizo* or *ladino* double consciousness is different somatically from the *criollo,* yet linguistically dissimilar from the Indigenous. The *mestizo* is not close to the European world, nor to the pre-Hispanic; his walk through history will be uncertain and, in a sense, lost, astray, given that he will contribute to the consolidation of internalised coloniality of power, knowing and doing.

Anglo-Saxon America, linked somatically and culturally to Europe is different from Latin America. The coloniality of power initiated in the sixteenth century would be consolidated itself here only in the nineteenth century, after the processes of independence. In this sense, Quijano points out that the second moment of coloniality of power is expressed in the construction of nation-states. The formation of the nation-state in Latin America is another expression of not only the coloniality of power but of the logic of the world-system as well. Quijano maintains that during the process of organising nation-states, the majorities of *mestizo*, Black and Indigenous people were excluded from the decisions made in such formations. The *criollo* core assumed control of those nation-states. The colonising paradigm moved from the Iberian peninsula to England, France and Germany. There was never really independence in the complete sense of the word, but rather a transfiguration in the colonial horizon.

The centrality of Europe in the world-system provoked the displacement of the colonial paradigm in Latin America. Europe's economic rise promoted the consolidation of the coloniality of power (formation of nation-states monopolised by a White minority), the coloniality of knowledge (ideologies of progress, enlightenment, evolutionism, etc.) and the coloniality of doing (citizenship, the urban, civics).

Anibal Quijano maintains that one of the clearest examples of this tragedy of mistakes in Latin America is the history of the so-called national question (2000: 226), given that its geopolitical peculiarities include the logic of cultural and political racism. The formation of the nation-states in Latin America strengthened the coloniality of doing and knowledge. The articulation of the world-system within the nation-states is paired to the logic of disciplining the Latin American population to the pattern of colonial domination.

The consolidation of the nation-states in the Latin American space was legitimised by the entelechy of inevitable transit towards modernity. The 'state of nature' becomes the 'political state' via geopolitically determined apparatus and institutions. For this reason, political organisation, such as the constitutions, was established to operate within a Western framework. The nation-state and its corollary, citizenship, exercised discipline on the doing of groups and individuals. At the dawn of the nineteenth century, the logic of power was transformed, showing that the forces of domination and resistance are not static, much less homogeneous.

De-indigenisation was commonplace and central in the Latin American project of national integration. The story of Benito Juárez in Mexico is perhaps the best example. A Zapotec Indian, he gained maximum power and took the presidency; as a Liberal, he read the classics, spent his exile in New Orleans, imitated the North American model and offered to surrender national sovereignty to Lincoln by signing the McLane-Ocampo Treaty. Not only that, Juárez de-indigenised himself completely by marrying Margarita Maza, daughter of the *patrón* of the house where his Zapotec Indian sister worked as a servant. Margarita Maza is *criolla* and Benito Juárez *zapoteco*; Juárez became the maximum expression of de-indigenisation: the Indian who at six years of age did not even speak Spanish and by much effort became president of the nation. The Zapotec Indian abandoned his culture, his language, his way of seeing the world and then stayed in the bosom of the oppressor's culture. Juárez's example signifies the denouncing of being Indigenous, a struggle against one's own blood. Another, equally pathetic example is found in the Ecuadorian president Gabriel García Moreno, also known as the 'Scaffold Saint'. During the middle of the nineteenth century García Moreno wanted to make Ecuador a French colony, and had the project of ethnically cleansing the country. Napoleon, however, did not accept this offer; nevertheless García Moreno dedicated his time to hosting Frenchmen, giving them lands and privileges.

The American Way of Life

Although its hegemony over the North Atlantic would become evident after the Second World War, when the United States took England's place in the world-system, the political and military presence of the North Americans in Latin America was already a fact. We cannot forget, for example, the war between the United States and Mexico in the middle of the nineteenth century, in which the latter lost half its territory.

Already by 1823, US President James Monroe declared in his seventh speech to Congress something that would mean catastrophe for Latin Americans: 'America for the Americans'. The intention, as we know, was to oppose geopolitically the interests of the Holy Alliance and the restoration of the monarchy in Europe. The declaration not only alienated the concept of *América*[34] but also revealed the aspirations and pretensions of the incipient North American empire.

The Monroe Doctrine served as the foundation of Yankee Manifest Destiny. Theodore Roosevelt[35] would use it as an inspiration for his foreign policy and *Realpolitik* dogma. John Gast's painting, *American Progress* (1872), notably expresses the meaning of such doctrine. In Latin America, the pattern of power relations, once directed by Europe, would now be configured according to the interests of North America. US hegemony would become evident in the world-system towards the end of the Second World War. The European Recovery Programme (ERP), also known as the Marshall Plan, was crucial to geopolitical rearrangement, given that it permitted the USA to impose itself as the new patron of world order. To this we add the 1944 creation of the World Bank and International Monetary Fund embodying the Bretton Woods agreement. The US dollar became the new imperial symbol. The centre of the world-system shifted towards North America (Wallerstein, 1999). According to Wallerstein, the Cold War, far from meaning the contraposition of two worlds diametrically opposed to one another, expresses the logic and dynamics of the world-system. For him, it was not a real struggle but a *compadrazgo*. Both powers possessed satellite countries (or colonies), defended the so-called self-determination of nations, believed in progress, the use of reason and development. Yankee hegemony began to displace nineteenth-century Eurocentrism and altered the civilising paradigm. In other words, it reconfigured the 'coloniality of power'.

One important book that covers and examines United States history, politics and its colonial background is Alexis de Tocqueville's *Democracy in America* (2000). With high tones of ethnocentrism and colonial cynicism, especially in chapter 10 – entitled 'Some considerations on the present state and probable future of the three races that inhabit the territory of the United States', Tocqueville (2000: 517) addresses the Indigenous question: 'Among such diverse men, the first who attracts attention, the first in enlightenment, in power, in happiness, is the white man, the European, man par excellence; below him appear the Negro and then the Indian.'

Tocqueville does not spare words of racism towards the Black people and Indians of the United States. For him, they are nothing more than animals or 'brutes' who have not yet developed a level of culture equal to that of the West. Progress in the United States, according to Tocqueville, is made by Western culture, product of the White man.

Postmodernity and Neoliberalism

It was during the 1970s that theoretical and aesthetic proposal of postmodernism emerged and with it the transformation of capitalism into its current form, neoliberalism. Latin America, especially Chile under the dictatorship of Augusto Pinochet, became the laboratory of elites experimenting with new projects of domination and exploitation. Nevertheless, dependency theory and liberation theology and philosophy demonstrated that the unequal relations between the centre and the periphery continued to be pronounced. The 'structural sin'[36] was denounced by its opponents, whose destiny was Río de Plata by way of the Death Flights (Dussel, 1977).

For his part, Lyotard (2000: 73) maintains that 'in contemporary culture and society … the question of legitimacy of knowledge arises in other terms. The grand narrative has lost its credibility, whatever the mode of unification to which it was assigned: speculative narrative, emancipation narrative.' The struggle for the radical transformation of social struggles became no longer pertinent, it was an anachronism. Revolution was no longer a social imperative but a discontinued metanarrative.

The depoliticised hermeneutic played into the one-track thinking. Likewise, the economy began to 'disarticulate'[37] itself from the political in the terrain of discourse. In order to comply with modernisation, perverse measures liberalising the national market were imposed upon the countries of the periphery. Instrumental reasoning of the world-system continued to provoke 'silent holocausts'.

Eclecticism is a feature particular to the postmodern culture – a sum of elements, according to the semiologist Omar Calabrese (1999), where all positions are assumed under different ethical parameters. That is to say, there is no uniformity, all is permitted. All can be conceived as 'aesthetic living or aesthetical experience',[38] from the killing on the streets of Brazil to humanitarian aid of the NGO-ist philosophy, or eco-tourism of Europeans of 'good conscience'. Lyotard (2005: 17–18) suggests that:

> eclecticism is ground zero of the general contemporary culture: we hear Reggae, we watch a Western, we eat at MacDonald's for lunch and a plate of local food at night, in Tokyo we perfume ourselves like in Paris, we dress ourselves in retro fashion in Hong Kong, knowledge becomes material for games on television … This realism is accommodated to all tendencies, as capital is adapted to all 'necessities', on the condition that the tendencies and the necessities have purchasing power.

But 80 per cent of the world's population lacks that power of purchase, and therefore it is an excessively restricted banquet.

Leonardo Boff (2000: 25) says that the postmodern proposal derives from the modern bourgeoisie. That is, 'the latest and most refined costume (*travestimento*) of capitalist culture with a consumerist ideology'. The lightness of postmodern judgement intends to sterilise popular demands, the calls for liberation and social change. For this reason, postmodernity and the New Age culture should be denounced as pillars of hegemonic logos.

Postmodernity is reduced to the hangman's reasoning[39] of differences or to the tools of extermination realised in a totalitarian project. However, it does not uphold its libertarian aspect, its challenging impulse, its revolutionary force. The role of reason should not be ignored by the people. On the contrary, it should be articulated in a project of social transformation.

Class and People[40]

In *Marx for our times* (2009), Daniel Bensaïd insists on working with the immanent contradictions of the system. As an historically defined social relation, capitalism has integrated different spheres of daily life under the logic of profit. The critique internal to the social dynamic is therefore not only legitimate but also urgent. The category of 'class' is essential for social analysis and the radical transformation of society. Enrique Dussel, in his *20 tesis de política* (2007a), and Leonardo Boff in his *A voz do arco-íris* (2000) claim the category of *pueblo* (people) in anti-hegemonic struggles. They do not discard the category of class, on the contrary they subsume it (*Aufgehoben*) into *pueblo*, the same way that Antonio Gramsci (2001: 182) did with the category 'subalternity'.

Although Marx did not use the term 'the people' when analysing 'capital as such', he does employ the term in his historical studies, conscious that the term 'class' is limited to the mode of capitalist production and reproduction, and therefore has a concrete historical imperative Dussel (2001: 187) argues that: '"Work" and "living labour" as non-capital (*Nicht Kapital*, as Marx liked to write) are absolute conditions of capital. But it is about "living labour" as "poor" not "salaried labor" (class); "work as absolute poverty"'. 'Living labour', before becoming salaried labour, and therefore 'working class', is poor simply due to the fact that capital is as yet non-existent, and cannot be considered some subsumed class. In addition, during that time preceding capital, when there is no money appearing as capital, nor a working 'class' (living labour as capital), there are the 'poor', and their socio-historical communitarian reference is 'the people' (*el pueblo*). In this manner, we note that the category *pueblo* is historically and analytically concordant with that of 'class'.

Without ignoring or negating the importance of material conditions and economic structure, Dussel (2007a) gives priority to the category '*pueblo*' at a political level, and even points to such a category as one that matches and is intimately linked to the 'social bloc of the oppressed'. *Pueblo* would be composed of the political community, where real political power lies. Power as *potential*, which would materialise in institutions (*potestas*) but that will have as its source the political power of the people. Therefore, the political community would be a place where full individuality and the complete collective would realise itself.

The Weberian oxymoron under the discursive figure of 'legitimate domination'[41] should be rethought under a new liberationist perspective where the immanent contradiction is revealed, as such an entelechy has only served to fetishise social relations under colonial categories and definitions. The people per se (*an sich*) is a fetishised and static moment, whereas people (*pueblo*) in its own right (*vor sich*) is converted into a dynamic process where the *consensus populi* is manifested, agreements are respected (*pacta servanda sunt*), in a word, 'the authorities command by obeying'. We should keep in mind the demarcation between the popular and populism, which lies at the political subject's locus of enunciation. Let me explain.

While 'popular' refers to the social bloc of the oppressed, the excluded and the wretched – in the Fanonian sense of the word, 'populism' refers to a clientelistic relation where a historical bloc in power makes use of social demands. The populist project lies at the antipodes of the contra-hegemonic project of the oppressed, as populism is a *telos* of domination that breaks the social flow, that fetishises social relations and under certain appearances conceals the logic of exploitation. For its part, the 'popular' project seeks the establishment of a 'new social contract', where the 'oppressed' is the subject of its own liberation.

The processes of independence, the struggles for decolonisation in Africa and the anti-systemic movements of Latin America[42] demonstrate that popular struggles are not delinked from the struggle against capital and its logic of exclusion. Class and *pueblo* can articulate themselves in the strategic discourses and in concrete tactics of subaltern groups. Class struggle is not only restricted to the process of production. Rather, it also permeates other spheres of life. However, the self-determination of peoples, respect for the other[43] and the re-politicisation of the economic is fundamental to the entire social project. In his *En defensa de la intolerancia* (Žižek, 2007) maintains that politics was born in Greece at a moment in which particularities kept outside of society generated a short circuit to universal hegemony. In any case, far from the Hellenic-centrism of this Slavic thinker, we believe that politics must be rethought and redefined from a liberationist perspective. *Liberationis conatus causa* should be our theoretical-practical locus.

Demanding Liberation

During the 1980s, those working in the field of Subaltern Studies revisited Gramscian contributions to historical and cultural analysis. Specifically, Ranajit Guha (2005) wrote on the temporal and discursive reductionism of the term 'class'. Classes and subaltern groups continued the struggle against capitalist ideology from the theoretical trenches positioned in the periphery: the postcolonial proposal. At another point in the periphery, the philosophy of liberation (inspired by the theology of liberation) would construct a narrative from the outside of the hegemonic system. The brutal dictatorships of Latin America, supported by international organisations such as the International Monetary Fund or the World Bank, acted as puppets of the neoliberal project. Under the doctrine of national security, the philosophy of liberation suffered exile, persecution and censure – proof of its political commitment to the oppressed.

Without renouncing social transformation and political struggle, the philosophy of liberation has proposed a project since the 1970s which was ethical, cultural, epistemic, political, economic, etc. based on principles and practical-discursive mediations which upheld human life, community and the conditions to sustain these. The cry of the poor and the Earth is central in such epistemic-political architecture.

From its locus of enunciation,[44] Liberation Philosophy has assimilated theoretical contributions of Western European, Arab-Muslim, Chinese, Sub-Saharan African and other thought, establishing both South–South and North–South dialogues in the critical currents of said geo-epistemic latitudes, demonstrating its universality and *trans-modernity* (Dussel, 2002).

The analectical method, the use of reason as an instrument of liberation (*ratio liberationis*) and the trans-modern project as a 'new alliance' (referring to the rainbow figure that Boff proposes, alluding to the construction of a 'new social contract' between human beings and nature, urgent and imperative for a post-capitalist society) of the victims of the system has been a valuable contribution to Latin American, critical political philosophy. Starting with non-being, the analectic is positioned beyond the boundaries and frontiers of Hegelian exclusionary dialectics because it begins with the physical suffering of the victims found among oppressed peoples. Reason is not vituperated against per se. On the contrary, its importance is revealed in its strategic use and is instrumental for the construction of a counter-hegemonic project. In contrast to postmodern reductionism, we claim reason as the arm of struggle against the system's fetishised truths. Trans-modernity can also be read under the proposal of *pluriversality* (Quijano, 2000), or eco-socialism (Löwy, 2005a), among others where the excluded are the preferential option.

We should restate some basic principles of social science, from the 'material negativity' of the victims, in order to realistically propose some lines in the construction of post-capitalist society, while keeping in mind that theoretical problems have practical consequences.

Exploitation and dispossession, as the motor of capital, should be combatted in all aspects of social life by a democratic-participatory form of organisation. At the same time, the bio-political discourse as the morality of the bloc in power should be confronted by an ethic of liberation. The revolutionary task and commitment should be on the side of the poor. The postmodern current emphasises the irrationality of reason and de-legitimises emancipation (Lyotard, 2000: 73). These represent dangerous lines of thinking in a global society where, according to the United Nations Development Programme (PNDU, 2008), more than 1 billion humans live on less than $1 a day, where 20 per cent of the world population monopolises 90 per cent of its resources (in 2003, they reported 80 per cent), where women earn 25 per cent less than men in similar jobs, where 30,000 children under the age of 5 die per day due to preventable illnesses.

The champions of postmodernity do not realise that emancipation, insubordination and revolution are ethical imperatives and social requirements. Two-thirds of humanity and the planet will not survive under this ecocide and exclusionary system. The struggle against capital is the struggle for life in all its manifestations. To not give up nor surrender in the political arena, as well as in the theoretical terrain, is to demonstrate our intolerance of such ideologies.

Permanent Conflict

Talcott Parsons's epistemic and political frustration at not being able to establish a triumvirate (Durkheim, Weber and Pareto), given that his intention was to exclude Karl Marx, is a commonplace in the history of sociology. In that respect, both Immanuel Wallerstein (1998) and Ruy Braga (Braga and Burawoy, 2008) maintain that, among the many contributions Marx made to social theory was his reflection on and reference to conflict.

It is worth mentioning that for Marx (2007) social reality is mediated by conflicts. Struggles between dominating groups (or classes) and subaltern groups (or classes), at all levels of reality, is a constant. On many occasions they are expressed in a clear fashion (revolutionary processes, boycotts, riots, among others), but they are always present. In this sense, a society that is asymmetrically organised is not exempt from tensions and ruptures. Totality, as a critical concept, continues to be valid and, as Žižek (2009: 76) would put it: this category does not refer to the occult harmony of the All but includes in the system all the symptoms – and therefore antagonisms and inconsistencies, as integral parts thereof. Here the social or cultural demands should not be delinked from the economic question, given that its omission could become an incentive to reify the system.

In Latin American and Caribbean history, the hegemonic (capitalist and colonial) system has designed different mechanisms of repression favourable to the elites, not only at the political-economic level but also culturally. Therefore, the phenomenon of violence as a structural component of capitalism cannot be avoided. Violence is not the result but an active element of capital.

In accordance with the Brazilian thinker Paulo Freire (1973: 49), we maintain that there would be no oppressed without the existence of a violent relation that violates them in an objective situation of oppression. It is those who oppress who have instituted the terror and structural violence; it is not the weak but the dominant elites. This imposed violence is a mechanism through which the dominating classes instil their own worldview. On the other hand, although it is evident that 'consensus' among the dominated plays an important role in the process of consolidating hegemony, we think that it is fundamental to analyse the relation between 'structural or imposed violence' and 'creative or liberating violence' in the socio-cultural dynamic of Latin America.

Independently of the imposition of different mechanisms of repression to maintain domination, subaltern groups rebel using a type of 'liberating violence'. In that respect, Frantz Fanon (2004) analysed the subjective process experienced by Algerians in their struggle for liberation, demonstrating that 'liberating violence' plays a part in the reconstitution of dominated subjects and peoples.[45] In this sense, Fanon claims the liberating effects that produce 'creative violence' in its ontological affirmation. In the same manner, C.L.R. James (2003: 94) makes note of 'violence' as expressed in *The Black Jacobins*, being that virulent momentary passion against the colonisers which was rapidly extinguished, given that its bitterness was not aimed at perpetuating the injustice but, on the contrary, destroying such a system of domination.[46]

The struggles for liberation of the Latin American and Caribbean periphery were not only directed towards imperialism and colonial capitalism but against the 'colonisation of power' in the broad sense of the word. For example, the slogan Ya Basta! of the Zapatista Army of National Liberation in the south-east of Mexico expresses the intention to heal some of the open veins in Latin American spaces, as well as to destroy the capitalist system and to de-fetishise politics. Neo-Zapatism fights a battle on different fronts: the struggle against savage capitalism brought to its maximum consequences (neoliberal globalisation), against the civilisational process that is superlative (Westernisation), against coloniality in elevated grades (cultural imperialism) and against the ideology of power at its extremes (one-track thinking). Above all, it also opposes colonial ontologies that developed hegemonic modernity.

Decolonising Power and De-fetishising Social Relations

The construction of the nation-state in Latin America did not translate into true independence for Afro-Caribbean and Indigenous groups. Unfortunately, the creation of states was articulated in the transfiguration of the modern world-system, which had as its axis France, Germany and England. Decolonisation failed and the countries of Latin America did not win economic and cultural independence. Throughout the nineteenth and twentieth centuries, the *criollo* elite administered dependent states, and therefore perpetuated the bases for a certain 'internal colonialism'.

Internal coloniality, interiorised by society as a whole, devalued popular culture. In that sense, we should understand Frantz Fanon (2004) when he postulated that in underdeveloped countries a real bourgeoisie does not exist. Rather, it is a species of lower caste with sharpened teeth, avid and voracious, dominated by the spirit of usury and which is content with the dividends that the colonial power assures him; these elites are thus caricatures of Europe.

Decolonisation would continue to be the pending task of Latin American societies. The forgotten of history, through defeats and failures, continued to learn and practise methods of organisation for the political, economic, social and cultural transformation of Latin America. It is no accident, then, that the peasants (Landless Workers Movement – MST) and the Indigenous peoples (Neo-Zapatista movement) have been the main protagonists of social struggle throughout the last 20 years.

The 1990s saw not only the attempt to consolidate the entelechies of the 'End of History' but also the continued implementation of structural adjustment programmes. The Washington Consensus was presented as a new objective discourse in the messianic narrative of power. The International Monetary Fund and the World Bank, therefore, played the role of vicars in the administration of globalisation's temporal terrain. Nevertheless, the MST and the Neo-Zapatista movements prophetically burst onto the scene as if they were bolts of lightning in history – as Walter Benjamin wrote (2001) – the figures that defy corrupted power. For this reason, the Neo-Zapatista movement represents one of the most relevant anti-systemic movements world-wide. Its struggle re-signified analytical categories, strategies of resistance and utopic horizons of civil organisations, militants and intellectuals of the world. Hence, recognition of its importance is fundamental in understanding the logic and dynamics of the hegemonic system and its structural contradictions.

From Uruguay, Raul Zibechi (2008: 85) argues that within the social movements of Latin America there exist forms of organisation characterised by these elements: (a) the politicisation of social and cultural differences, in other words, lifestyles; (b) the crisis of representation expressed in the lack of confidence in clientelistic and bureaucratic politics; (c) non-statehood or, better yet, the transcendence of the state-centric horizon; and (d) diversity in the forms of struggle, or moments of social insubordination, highlighting without doubt the roadblocks set up by protesters and communities of resistance. Such resistance takes many shapes, from the form of production of a company taken by workers in the south of Argentina to Indigenous uprisings in Ecuador, through the resistance of the Mapuche people, the Other Campaign of the Zapatistas, to the experience of the *agrovilas* of the MST in Brazil and their pedagogical critique, to name only a few. Furthermore Zibechi (2008) underscores the lack of confidence demonstrated by the social movements towards traditional ways of doing politics, given that on occasion the left has betrayed popular interests. Take Mexico's Party of Democratic Revolution (PRD), for example, when they rejected the Indigenous Rights and Culture Law in 2001, or the co-option of some leaders of the Worker's Party (PT) under the presidency of Luis Inazio 'Lula' da Silva. It is worth remembering that Frei Betto, a renowned liberation theologian, who at one time led the state-run programme Zero Hunger, decided to distance himself from Lula's cabinet from 2004 (Aguirre Rojas, 2008: 49).

Another interesting feature of the social movements of Latin America, especially the MST of Brazil and the Neo-Zapatista movement in Mexico, is related to the role of women. The feminisation of social struggle impregnated not only the spatial-temporal mesh of the movements but also the performative logic of their demands, which results in 'another way' of concretising emancipatory practices. Going beyond the superficial focus of multiculturalism, Zibechi (2008: 269) recognises the impact of the role of the woman-mother on anti-systemic logic and states that: 'with them, there erupts another rationality, another culture, a relational episteme'.

Popular struggle in Latin America cannot be simply analysed from a Eurocentric perspective; this applies to traditional sociological and positivist approaches, as well as those of classical Marxists or the failed postmodern theories of culture, as the endogenous dynamic of Latin American processes deserve the use of concepts and categories that are closer to our loci of enunciation, and our position in material and symbolic production. In that respect, we should understand Eduardo Galeano (2009: 37) when he writes about the MST in Brazil, saying:

> One afternoon in 1996, nineteen landless peasants were shot in cold blood by members of the military police of Pará state in the Brazilian Amazon. In Pará and in much of Brazil, the lords of the land reign over empty vastnesses, thanks to the right to inheritance or the right to thievery. These property rights give them the right to impunity. Ten years after the massacre, no one is in jail. Not the lords, not their thugs. But the tragedy did not frighten or discourage the landless farmers. The membership of their organisation mushroomed, and so did their will to

work the land, even though that is a capital offense and act of incomprehensible madness.

Analysing the Neo-Zapatistas in Mexico and the MST in Brazil, Raúl Zibechi (2008: 24) finds seven common features or ethical-political characteristics that underlie their dynamic: (a) the territorial roots of the movements, that is, the space in which the community is ontologically and materially reproduced; (b) autonomy as a form of organisation, implying distrust of the clientelistic practices of the state and political parties; (c) the cultural revaluation of their identities, that is, beyond the Eurocentric category of citizenship; (d) the appropriation and decolonisation of knowledge represented in the formation of their own cadres and intellectual currents; (e) the role of women in the re-creation of another organisational logic; (f) the relation with nature, and, finally, (g) the self-affirmative forms of re-appropriating public spaces represented in the taking over of cities, the settlements (in the case of MST) and places of memory.

The Neo-Zapatista insurrection revived popular struggle and gave a new grammar to the discourse of social movements. Reference to 'all the peoples of the world' from the start unveiled the global significance and internationalist spirit of the Neo-Zapatista movement. That internationalism, however, did not divert them from their national objectives (with respect to the San Andrés Accords, the installation of a true democracy, and respect for the customs and practices of original nations, etc.) and their fundamental interests (the destruction of capitalism, the decolonisation of the state and respect for the environment).

Agrarian reform plays an important part in these social conflicts that underlie Latin American reality. Thus Zibechi recuperates the transcendence of the material and subjective question of land and the social imaginary. It is not by accident that, in the triad formulated by the author (territory, self-governance and autonomy), land is central when highlighting the dynamic of emancipation. The insurgent Subcomandante Marcos once remarked in an interview that an Indigenous people without land is not Indigenous, as their language and the like are disrupted; if land is destroyed the Indigenous no longer have roots, it would be like killing their family. For his part, João Pedro Stedile (2005: 44) declared that the MST struggle for agrarian reform was a struggle for all, given that it is struggle against neoliberalism.

The Zapatistas reclaim and instate a society where direct democracy becomes pillar of collective agreement. At the plane of material production, they also advocate for respect for nature and the environment. For them, autonomy in the face of the state and the market is paramount.[47] Some of the organising points of the MST in Brazil are based on: collective leadership, division of tasks, discipline, study, the formation of cadres, the struggle for land (agrarian reform) and links with the bases. In this sense, the MST's social and political project leans towards radical democracy of society and a non-commercial relation with nature.

Marcelo Barros and Frei Betto (2009: 93–94), related how, in the early 1980s, Peruvians waited anxiously for Pope John Paul II's visit to Latin America. On that occasion, in the old city of Cuzco, the Pope met with some Indigenous people; among them, they recall, was a Yatari elder of the Andes who, approaching the pontiff, said:

> Holy Father, my people and I are thankful for your visit. I never thought that one day I would see the pope of Rome. We know that you have come to speak about God and share with us his words and wisdom. We receive it delightfully. But we wanted to say that your ancestors, the Europeans who arrived 500 years ago brought us this Bible. We received it in good faith but did not know that they gave us the Bible in exchange for land. Now, I have come in the name of my people to return the Bible and ask that my lord demand that the descendants of Europeans return our lands.

We believe that neo-colonial projects are manifested in different aspects of social reality, at the political level, in the socio-economic spectrum and undoubtedly in cultural spaces. Therefore, the aftermath of the North American civilising paradigm should be scrutinised in order to effect a radical rupture with colonial atavism. The hegemony of North Atlantic imperialism has driven, via globalisation as a political-military strategy, its project of re-colonialisation in the Latin American space. The commercialisation of social relations, the MacDonaldisation of culture (Ritzer, 1999) and the fetishisation of power has made inequality and social injustice more acute.

Undeniably, social processes are mediated by power relations, that is, their dynamic is configured by struggles, tensions and conflicts. Reality is not static, much less is it one-dimensional; we must recognise its active and contradictory character. We are convinced, however, that the patterns of control, domination and exploitation are constantly being transfigured; hence domination, power and resistance should be conceived as processes in perpetual transformation.

The Pandora's Box, opened in Latin America and the Caribbean at the threshold of the sixteenth century, gave forth the modern world-system, the advent of a modern colonial imaginary and the imposition of a 'coloniality of power' (Quijano, 2001), of knowledge (Mignolo, 2003) and of 'doing' geopolitics. The configuration of the civilising triad (capitalism/ modernity/coloniality) should be analysed and contextualised in an articulate manner. A break with cultural dependency and gnoseological submission to colonial horizons should be both a political and epistemic demand. Therefore, concepts such as the state of nature, civilisation, progress, development or evolution, among many others, should be deconstructed from a critical analectical and liberating starting point, given that the locus of enunciation from our point of view should be consistent with our geopolitical as well as our cultural context.

2

The Shopping Mall as the Paradigmatic Figure of Necolonial Discourse: Racism and Power in Latin America[1]

In social reality, the processes of fetishisation and de-fetishisation (resistance and struggle) are composed of multiple discourses that legitimise, strengthen and configure them with the break from domination. The constitution of social reality is constantly being transformed, due to conflict, tensions and shifts between power(s) and counter-power(s). However, after more than five centuries of imperial, colonial and capitalist domination and exploitation, we observe that the political asymmetry, economic inequality and ethno-racial injustice have become more acute in peripheral societies. Is it possible that the 'structural sin' – to borrow a term from the theologists of liberation – continues to take its toll on the souls of the oppressed in the Third World?

The colonial paradigms and the logic of capital have set the pace for hegemonic discursive practices in Latin America. Power, knowledge and doing have been tainted by the dominant *telos* of imperial powers. The geopolitical and cultural consequences of neo-colonialism are re-packaged in the context of globalisation, militarisation, the commercialisation of life (McDonaldisation) and ecocide.[2] The current world-system has created an asymmetric society where 20 per cent of the world's population controls-consumes 80 per cent of the resources. Levels of poverty have increased by 100 per cent. Economic disparity between the countries of the North and those of the South are despicable. The 'humiliatocracy'[3] (*halloukratia*) of the imperial powers, its projects of neo-colonialisation and its civilising discourses deserve a 'liberating deconstruction' from

peripheral critical theorists. In order to do that, we shall deconstruct one
of the most representative discursive objects in the neo-colonial narrative:
the (shopping) mall – because it is linked to the logic of capital.

To analyse the role of shopping malls in the process of neo-
colonialisation in Latin America implies revealing how certain discursive
objects of the modern narrative, born in the sixteenth century, operate in
the social imaginary of the population today. For example, 'civilising' ideas
that counterpoise those of barbaric, backward and grotesque societies;
a class habitus that supports what appears to be a new system of castes
and reconfigured colonial myths can be discerned in the ideological
enunciations of certain social groups.

The first shopping malls appeared in the United States during the
twentieth century.[4] Their teleological function consists of warehousing,
storing, promoting and selling merchandise under a new logical framework.
Publicity, ads and mass media would be important factors in the making of
these showcases of happy promises and dreams of possession.[5]

The mushrooming of shopping malls began in the 1950s. The countries
of the centre did not spare resources in the construction of these temples
of capital. Marcuse's *one-dimensional man* entered the stage and the society
of mass consumption expressed the social hegemonic form. Analyses from
the Frankfurt School demonstrated that mass consumption contributed
to the reification of the capitalist system. For Marcuse, the population
witnessed and abided by the homogenisation of bourgeois values by way
of fun and leisure. Mass culture transformed social subjectivity and, in
this sense, gestated a semantic continuity (imaginary) making uniform
tastes, preferences and antipathies. Culture became consumption and
merchandise turned into poetic figures.

The presence of shopping malls in Latin America became more
common. Director of the Inter-American Council of Shopping Centres for
Mexico and Central America, Xavier Pumarejo, reported that Mexico was
ranked in first place in the development of shopping malls throughout
Latin America. In 2004, US$ 1.4 billion was invested in the creation of
new shopping centres throughout the country. For its part, the Promotora
y Desarrolladora Company, whose partners are the consortium Ara
and O'Connor Capital Partners (founded by Jery O'Connor, who built
more than 30 malls in the USA), invested $US 100 million towards the
development of shopping centres in the country. Mall experts show that
conditions for the opening of shopping centres are most favourable when

there is demonstrable interest from foreign financial institutions and high competition among supermarket chains, department stores and cinemas.

The shopping mall, as a discursive object in the colonial narrative, deserves to be analysed given that its presence reveals the transfiguration of the pattern of control, domination and cultural exploitation. From a critical perspective we shall try to unravel the ideological *telos* of the current civilisational paradigm. Although the Latin American reader might think that this phenomenon is one that belongs to Mexico, together with the philosopher of Trier: *de te fabula narratur*!

Consumption and Geopolitically Defined Distinction

Undoubtedly, the process of globalisation has generated a symbolic-cultural exchange among nations. It is necessary to point out, nevertheless, that in some cases this exchange has been imposed by cultures belonging to the core. The relevance of Colonial Studies lies in revealing the forms and mechanisms of invasion/imposition of worldviews (*Weltanschauungen*) by imperial powers on the periphery. Capitalism is not only a mode of production, it is at the same time a specified social relation (Marx, 2007). To analyse the processes of this social form implies recognising the dynamics and logic of its works. The study of its manifestations, in this case consumption, should be contextualised and correlated to the hegemonic *telos*.

Towards the end of the nineteenth century, Thorstein Veblen wrote his famous *Theory of the leisure class* (1974) to demonstrate the ostentatious practices of the dominant classes.[6] We find Veblen's work attractive in that it suggests an analysis of consumption and its relation to the processes of social distinction. Veblen (1974) analyses the differences between aristocratic or conspicuous activities and industrial or popular activities (barbarian culture). For Veblen, conspicuous consumption and conspicuous leisure denotes the prestige and honour of individuals. The relation between leisure and consumption is fundamental to modern society and in the configuration of social classes.

Consumption, as an expression of social position, is paramount among the customs of social classes. For example, while the dominant classes (the leisure classes) boast of their waste and squandering of resources, the popular classes are discreet in the administration of their resources. The first seek prestige more than usefulness, while the popular classes must skimp their costs. Thus Veblen analyses such diverse aspects of social life as music, sports, fashion and food, among others, in order to reveal the differences in the acquired tastes of social classes. Discursive practices or manners, as Veblen would put it, express capital culture; that is to say, all of the intellectual qualities produced by the school system or transmitted through the family individually and among social classes. It is important to state here that, for Veblen, the dominant classes impose norms, rules, conventionalisms and canons of behaviour.

Of course Veblen's thesis should be contextualised geopolitically, given that its potentiality resides in unveiling the logic of distinction among social classes. For him, the habits and customs make manifest the social position of individuals. In the peripheral sphere of structural inequality we notice that discursive practises lean towards the pattern of colonial domination and express submission to the civilisational horizon.

In Latin America since the sixteenth century, colonial paradigms have shaped societal power, knowledge and doing. Discursive practices uphold such civilising references as the behaviour and manners of foreign societies and, therefore, the socio-cultural imaginary has been coloured by the incumbent metropolis. The coloniality of doing is present in the social relation of the Latin American periphery. Discursive practices seek not only to enunciate social classes but stages of civilisation as well. The benchmark is the imperial narrative and the colonial entelechies.

Published in 1979, Bourdieu's *La Distinction* (2002a) presents a thorough and rigorous study of the social distribution of cultural tastes. Basing himself on a survey of French society, Bourdieu tried to demonstrate that cultural practices comprise the base of varying social groups and, therefore, represent the underlying principle of social difference. *Distinction* displays a process of political domination in the cultural sphere, and we can observe substantial symbolic conflict among social groups. The teleological function of the conflict is not simple domination, nor to defend orthodoxy (patterns of beauty, aesthetic canons and discursive norms); rather, it is to create social differences in order to maintain the distinctiveness of social groups. The logic of cultural practices is not free or spontaneous, given that it is inscribed into social history and should be understood as something that serves the dominant culture. It is important to state here that the cultural practices of agents are inseparable from the theory of domination and therefore, following Bourdieu (2002a), it is through culture that the dominant classes assure their position.

According to Bourdieu, good taste (*bon goût*), exquisite thought (*belle pensée*) and beautiful expression (*beau parler*) are defined by domination; that is, they respond to laws of the system of exclusion. We should recognise here that it is those social groups equipped with high cultural capital that visit museums, go to the opera and populate the libraries. Access to cultural goods is unequal and is yet another expression of the asymmetrical relations of the hegemonic social form.

The main hypothesis of *Distinction* is that cultural practices such as institutional schooling have the function of assigning status – that is, creating a logic of classification (*logique de classement*) of agents in social spaces. In other words, cultural practices comprise the materialisation of an incorporated historical process and become the expression of a certain habitus. Bourdieu analyses the distinction between the refined taste (*goût cultivé*) of high culture (*haute culture*) and popular taste (*goût populaire*) in order to denounce the hypocrisy of the dominant classes. While the pure taste of elites does not emphasise usefulness, the anti-Kantian aesthetics of popular taste gives primacy to function over form. The habitus or disposition of an event becomes the sedimentation of a *doxa* or an acquired *hysteresis* through schooling, the family and (we add) culture. The structural relation between cultural practices is in itself an expression of class struggle, and therefore the discursive practices are classified according to the field[7] in which they are inscribed. To contextualise Veblen (1974) and Bourdieu (2002a) geopolitically, we can observe that, in Latin America, the process of social difference is not only cultural but civilisational. In other words, the logic of classifying responds to the colonial imaginary. To distinguish oneself from a social group is, at the same time, to place oneself at a specific civilisational stage.

Castro-Gómez (2000) has pointed out that just as there is a direct relation between language and citizenship, there is also a relation between the grammars and ordinances of urban life in the construction of the modern/colonial imaginary. For Castro-Gómez the normativity of letters and grammars seeks to generate a culture of good talk (*beaux parler*) in order to avoid the low-class practices of popular parlance and gross barbarism of the plebs. The civilised man knows how to eat, speak, dress, write, walk, etc. in a sophisticated way. *En fin*, his doing is what distinguishes him from the popular classes, from the undesirable, from the Others.

The process of social distinction in the Latin American periphery responds to the logic and patterns of colonial behaviour. The coloniality of doing has consolidated cultural dependency and the symbolic domination of central powers. In this sense, discursive practices express not only a geopolitical imposition but also a latent conflict among peoples and between worldviews.

The Cathedral of Brands and the Mecca of Merchandise

The shopping mall has become the place of imperial symbols (logos and brands) of hegemonic narratives. Vattimo (1998a) qualifies it as the dominion and unification of the planet. The mall is a cathedral of brands, the Mecca of merchandise and the temple of capital; it is the most ominous expression of the *pauper ante festum*. The commonplace of imperial signs and apotheosis is headquartered at commercial centres. Its presence and *raison d'être* necessitates the imposition of models, images and discursive figures in contemporary times. From Harrods to Lafayette, we find common discursive objects given that certain brands, logos and merchandise are familiar within different social niches.

Jean Baudrillard (2005) maintains that consumer society can be understood as a host of signs, given that the objects (Baudrillard, 2003) form a discourse. For this author, the social system is a complex of signs (denotative) and symbols (connotative) in constant tension, and, like Veblen, he holds that the dynamic of consumption is an ostensible logic of difference. Baudrillard (2002) is convinced that an object (merchandise) abridges four logics. First, the functional logic of the use of value, which is governed by usefulness; second, mercantile logic or exchange value ruled by equivalence and the market; third, symbolic value, which refers to talent, reciprocity and the determinations of the symbolic; fourth and last, the differential logic of signs, which establish status and hierarchies. He then proceeds to analyse consumption in two dimensions: the symbolic aspect on the one hand, and on the other the process of classification and social distinction.

In consumer society, says Baudrillard (2005), one attempts to buy happiness (*bonheur*) and the idea of the individual is fundamental in this imaginary. Alienation and consumption form a system of self-referenced signs where the individual becomes a vehicle of objects. Baudrillard sees the body (*corps*) as the most beautiful object of consumption. He demonstrates that current structures of production/consumption bring the subject's body to a double practice. One the one hand as capital, and on the other as a fetish (2005: 200). The body is revealed as a central object in the narrative of capital. Its re-appropriation is not an autonomous end in itself; rather it is a normative principle of hedonistic profitability. Hence, Baudrillard considers those under extravagant beauty care to be more alienated than simply the exploited bodies of the workforce. The body is a sign and therefore expresses social differentiation. The hegemonic narrative considers the body to be a walking commercial which serves to advertise its imperial signs. To use his language, we can say that brand names and logos give added value to the body.

For Naomi Klein (2001), throughout recent years, capital has invested more in advertising than in the quality of products. Serving as the image of a company, the logo is at the same time a sign with characteristics of other discursive elements. The logo and the brand name possess semiotic characteristics that designate status; that is, they actively participate in the process of social differentiation.

At the shopping malls we can find imperial signs (brand names and logos of transnational capital) of the colonial account. Products and merchandise designate social status and, at the same time, unequal structure among nations. The paradigmatic of doing is restricted by the patterns of geopolitical domination and exploitation marked by central powers. In other words, commercial centre dynamics express a world market logic, grounded in an asymmetrical economy and political imbalance.

The imperial signs (brands and logos) of 'postmodern' merchandise – as Lyotard[8] calls it, appear to us as a magnanimous process of social refinement. However, it would be interesting to ask ourselves about the mystery of their production. Naomi Klein demonstrated that the large transnational corporations do not possess their own factories where products are made. Rather, they rely on contractors that supply them with merchandise at a low price. The work that is done in the countries of the core has been made more intensive and forms the scaffolding for the economies of the peripheral nations. Work in the *maquiladoras* – or export processing zones, as Klein calls them – is another expression of the modern, neo-colonial and capitalist world-system form of production, as it extracts objectified labour as well as resources and raw materials from the inhabitants of the periphery … not to mention the ecocide that this process has induced.

The neoliberal fallacy indicates that *maquiladoras* contribute to the economic and social development of countries fighting poverty. A closer look, however, would reveal that it is precisely this process that enhances the gap between rich and poor. Centre–periphery relations continue to be present in the dynamic of capital and, in this sense, the coloniality of power is hinged to the world-system. As Wallerstein (1991: 108) points out: 'The fact is that historical capitalism has been up to now a system of very differential rewards, in both class and geographical terms.'

At the *maquiladoras*, the discursive objects of the colonial narrative are produced by pain and, in some cases, by blood.[9] These export processing zones are hidden (as is their value) yet are fundamental for the transnational corporations. In this sense, and going beyond Baudrillard, we think that there is a logic added to the merchandise and it is a dynamic of structural asymmetry. Behind the sideboards and brands there is not only one process of objectification of labour but an entire historical practice of material exploitation in the periphery.

The following is an eloquent testimony related to what we are talking about. On 13 February 2006, during the Zapatista 'Other Campaign', Delegate Zero (insurgent Subcomandante Marcos), visited the community of San Miguel Tzinacapan of Cuetzalan municipality in Pueblo, Mexico. There, he went to listen to the victims of the neoliberal capitalist system. *Maquiladora* workers talked about the injustices, violations and abuses to which they are subjected by *principium oppressionis* of the ruling class. Delegate Zero related the merchandise objects of capitalist discourse to the pains of the workers; that is to say, the objectification of value found in imperial signs:

> when we buy a pair of pants, for example, we don't see what's going on. The history of exploitation given by our *compañeras* and *compañeros* is not written on a label. The 12-hour work days are not reported on the pair of pants; nor is the humiliation prompted by line managers or foremen expressed; nor the exploitation of those victims after a day shift, who only receive a small amount of money. Here is the wangle of the system. Products appear but those who produced them, who suffered to make them don't appear. And most of all, where do these products go? Not to the one who produced the merchandise, not to the *compañera* or *compañero* who sewed those pants, who dyed them and who put on the label. It is for the business owner. And perhaps that owner happens to be one of those big politicians or related to one of those big politicians who lives in Tehuacán valley and whose family name is Gil. And perhaps if we scratch further beyond those names

we might find the names of large corporations from other countries. On those pants a hidden story is written, about when they were dyed blue and with the residues of the dye the water of Tehuacán valley was contaminated; and at the hour of contamination, the Indigenous people and the communities dependent on the water springs were affected by the contamination. And at the hour of losing water and land, they had to migrate to the United States, to look for work over there. And they walk through one of those large cities of the United States and see in the department stores these very same pair of pants with an American brand on them, prices in dollars; they know that those pants were made by their families here ... Just imagine if every piece of merchandise that we buy carried the history of worker exploitation suffering, humiliation. And then, each piece of merchandise would turn into an agitator that would be saying that there is no justice in this country ... On those jeans history will be written, not only the history of exploitation but of rebellion, the one that began in Altepexi in 2006, and, together with all those who stood up in the rest of the country, illuminated Mexico and gave it the most beautiful lesson that these lands were ever given: that those who struggle together with others may have justice, democracy and liberty. (Bellinghausen, 2006; original translation)

Modernity, Hegemony and the Process of Exclusion

Michel Foucault (2005) suggests that modernity should not be thought of as emancipation but as another form of repression, as its modus operandi is the constant negation of a certain Otherness.[10] For Foucault, all discourse is inscribed into a series of laws that coerce, lead, constrain and, in a sense, he suggests that the production of discourse is controlled in all societies.

Modern discourse is overrun by relations of power which consolidate three systems of specific exclusion: the prohibited, the diametrically opposed relation between reason (*raison*) and craziness (*folie*), and the binomial vision of truths and untruths. In addition, the process of disciplining is fundamental in the order of discourse (*ordre du discours*). Discipline and power are intimately related in the modern imaginary, given that they are materialised in control over the spirit and the body. For this reason, Foucault distinguished two types of bio-power: the politics of anatomy, which refers to docile bodies, and bio-politics, represented by the control of populations, territories, public spaces, etc. Following

Foucault, we can say that discipline applies not only to bodies, space and time, it also legitimises the policing of discourse. In this sense we maintain that the existence of a disciplined society is imperative to modern forms of domination and exploitation.[11]

For his part, Henri Lefebvre (1971) points to space as being the product of socio-historical relations, just as Marx wrote about the production of merchandise; that is, that all products contain and dissimulate certain social relations. François Chesnais and Claude Serfati (2003: 102) note that the history of capitalism has taught us that the bourgeoisie does not construct space for economic purposes only, but for the political objective of preventing the working class, in its concentrated space, from finding the necessary force for its emancipation.

From his 'geographical-historical materialism', David Harvey (1998) argues that although modernity and postmodernity are antithetical, there exist numerous continuities between them. If there was a superficial change in capitalism from 1973 onwards, the subjacent logic of the obtaining of benefits and the tendency of the crisis continues to be the same. For Harvey, the move towards Fordism and the regime of flexible accumulation is fundamental in the process of spatial-temporal transformation. For this reason the shopping malls, where fashion prevails, express the dynamic of instantaneous capital which is transient, volatile and fragmented in images, discourses and narratives. Time and space is the knot that ties together the processes in economic and cultural changes with the same teleological dynamic: the reproduction of the capitalist mode of production. It is as if for Harvey, modernity and postmodernity are metamorphosed continuities in cultural-aesthetic opposing categories.

At the malls, there exists a process of discipline and social control. Its spatial organisation is planned with areas of food (fast food or restaurants), for example, at a specific place. Territory, as Foucault mentions, should be organised according to normative principles which assure the regularity of discourse; that is, the relations of power dictate 'the order of things and its discourse'. Therefore, we can note a specific calculation, mediated by capital, in the spatial-temporal organisation of commercial centres.

The discursive practices that are established between subjects at the shopping malls in Latin America are ruled geopolitically by patterns of colonial powers. The mall consolidates hegemonic narratives of domination, the McDonaldisation of society and the unification of the planet. Resistances and struggles against these forms of domination should be analysed and articulated in political (Fanon, 2004), ethical (Dussel, 2003) and epistemic (Santos, 2003) projects of social transformation. To challenge one-track thinking requires individual-collective efforts, and for this our gnoseological, existential and ontological horizon should go towards and beyond social liberation.

From the trenches of pain suffered by the victims of capital, the imperial signs have been and are being challenged. As the French peasant confederation (Confédération paysanne) has shown us, in this context, even eating becomes a political act.[12] The alter-globalisation movement has taught us that even in the act of organisation there is a ludic moment, and the Zapatista Indigenous movement showed us that insurgency is an ethical, vital and dignified imperative. The break with civilising horizons and colonial narratives should be a political and epistemic demand. The rebellious dignity of the oppressed and hope – as a principle of the condemned of these lands – continue to nourish the questions to be answered along the path of struggle.

The theoreticians of power of the core, as well as the colonised intellectuals of the periphery have proposed the term 'postcoloniality' to refer to a historical period in which territorial occupation and domination of one nation by another has been overcome.[13] However, by postcoloniality – as Mignolo (2001: 16) would say – we do not infer the disappearance but the mutation and transformation of the patterns of exploitation, domination and control. Although nations express sovereignty in their constitutions, the colonial system continues to operate in the logic of social relations. There can be no doubt that ruptures and negations have been present in this social plot; the mechanisms of control, domination and exploitation still exist.

The aim of analysing symbolic-cultural coloniality is to demonstrate that the articulated neoliberal project masks a discourse of Western, imperial control/domination which proposes a civilising process (Dussel, 2013) as a goal to be reached in the corporeal, ontological and linguistic sense. The Moroccan Mahdi Elmandjra (2004: 35) warns us of the dangers of this civilisational crusade (*guerre civilisationnelle*) in the social imaginary of the world population.

The project of colonisation is driven from the core-powers through such diverse ideological mechanisms of control/domination as television, radio, newspapers and the internet, that the youth of the peripheral nations apprehend with the purpose of feeling included in the civilising process.[14]

Corporeality and Socialisation

Reflection on corporeality has been absent in Western thought. According to Enrique Dussel (2013: 34), Hellenic anthropological dualism, with its corresponding contempt for the body, sensitivity, passion and sexuality, subsequently penetrated gnostic-Roman traditions, Latin Manichaeism, the beliefs of Albigensians and the Cathars, also influencing Descartes (a disincarnated *ego*) and Kant. In that respect Dussel holds that:

> the empirical, corporeal or appetitive is for Kant 'the pathological' as the human being belongs to 'two worlds', that of the spirits and that of souls with bodies. This dualism is based on extreme universalist, rationalist formalisms; that is, ignorance of corporeality and therefore obliviousness of the economic. (2013: 47)

Hence we think it necessary to make note of social aspects of corporeality.

Corporeality should analytically be considered fundamental to social relations. Far from falling into empiricisms without relations, we think that the analysis of corporeality should lay out new questions for philosophy and social thought. The body is a carrier of phylogenetic cellular processes as well as cultural histories. To concretise this thought with an 'apparently' irrelevant example, we believe that it is not the same being a North African or Helvetic in Europe, as it is different being Lacandon or Mapuche rather than *criollo* in Latin America.

Within the analytical framework of the philosophy of perception proposed by Maurice Merleau-Ponty (1998), the concept of *a priori corporal* refers to somatic capital that determines a specific place of enunciation. It can be summarised in the idea that we are our bodies; that is, our body, a concrete entity, marks and is marked by specific social processes.

Theodor W. Adorno, in his negative philosophy, states that: 'without body there is no being' (1990: 139); that is, all ontology needs a factual or ontic foundation for thought about being. For this reason, analysis of hegemonic corporeality is a condition sine qua non in Colonial Studies. Hegemonic corporeality is aesthetically valid for the actual system; it represents the beautiful, the attractive, the canons of being, as opposed to the ugly, the unpleasant and the grotesque. Sigifredo Marín (2006: 8) writes that: 'recent debates allude, explicitly or implicitly, to the body and its representations. In the streets or on television a dictatorship of a series of canons of beauty can be perceived, which structure (while deconstructing) our subjectivity.'

In the colonial context of the periphery, the corporeal capital of White individuals is superior to that of *mestizos*, Black people and Indigenous peoples. At the plane of racial stratification, White people are found at a privileged place of enunciation. The locus of enunciation – which is determined by the *a priori corporal* – is fundamental to the social relations of the periphery. This intuition of corporeality and its identity with being is found in the Western philosophy expounded by the Lithuanian-French thinker Emmanuel Levinas. In *Humanism of the other*, he brings to an extreme Merleau-Ponty's idea that: 'our bodies are the delegates of being' (2001a: 33). Levinas, however, does not stop here. If the body is the delegate of being, that same being is unveiled only and absolutely by its face. 'The face has purpose, not for its relations but from itself' (2001b: 87). In this sense, the face is a complex carrier of knowledge, a manifestation of totality. Being as it is, an immense arsenal of phenotypes, and genetic, somatic and ontological information, Levinas cannot conclude differently than to say: 'the face is the presentation of an entity, his persona presentation' (2001b: 87).

The face is, first and foremost, the place where 'I' takes consciousness of the Other. It might be interesting, after such a statement, to think of the Other from a privileged place of enunciation. Levinas speaks from Western and Renaissance ontology, in which man is White, Christian and Civilised. According to Dussel, Levinas 'never thought that the Other could be Indigenous, African or Asian' (Mignolo, 2001: 29). In Levinas' European philosophy, the Other is uniquely and exclusively the Jew. Under the shadow of Kant and Hegel, Western-colonial intellectuals radically hide and negate the Other. This negation situates the Black person, the Latin American, the colonised in a position of ultimate exclusion, in a wilderness that goes way beyond the ontological border in the field of non-being.

If, in reality, the Other is Latin American, African, the colonised, the poor, the oppressed, the wretched of the Earth, and if the being is unveiled in the face, what, then, does the face of that radically different Other tell us? Enrique Dussel (1985: 44) responds to this question:

The face of the other, primarily as poor, oppressed, reveals a people before it reveals an individual person. The brown face of the Latin America *mestizo* wrinkled with the furrows of centuries of work, the ebony face of the African slave, the olive face of the Hindu, the yellow face of the Chinese coolie is the irruption of the history of a people … Each face, unique, inscrutable mystery of decisions not yet made, is the face of a sex, a generation, a social class, a nation, a cultural group, a historical epoch.

The first thing that the face reveals is race, which is, according to Anibal Quijano (1998, 2000, 2001), one of the founding pillars of world capitalist, modern/colonial and Eurocentric patterns of power. This idea of race is linked directly to the socio-historical division of labour: the White is salaried, the other races are inferior for the European totality, they are not worthy of such salary. In the colour of their skin, these races express their destiny – servitude. Hence the popular maxim: 'Work like a Black person to live like a White man.'

Analysing hegemonic corporeality in Latin America allows us to observe the internalisation of the canons of beauty and the prescriptions of what is aesthetically valid in a context of colonial continuity. Race, body and face are determinants in social relations of the periphery,[15] and we must therefore consider inescapable the notion of corporeal capital.

Corporeal capital, as a central element in coloniality – of power and doing – in Latin America configures and sustains the social relations that it produces, establishes and reproduces in a context of power asymmetry and social inequality.

Pierre Bourdieu points out that the habitus classifies the actor who classifies and the habitus also classifies the very function of distinguishing between the different classifications. The analytical pertinence of habitus is its logic of cultural classification of social classes. However, to contextualise such an analytical tool geopolitically, we are obliged to propose the concept of corporeal capital. Corporeal capital as a conceptual tool allows for the revealing of geopolitical specificities in the social relations of the Latin American periphery. Undoubtedly, the concept should be outlined and contextualised geo-analytically. In short, we define corporeal capital as: phenotype characteristics and somatic features that determine the locus of enunciation in geopolitically specified social-cultural relations. Corporeal capital limits, distinguishes, classifies and empowers the habitus of the actor.

We approach this concept of socialisation defined as forms and attitudes of individuals in relation to their socio-cultural environment: in other words, the subject's way of acting with other people. Socialisation implies breaks and negativities; that is, conflicts between subjects and worldviews. However, being embedded in asymmetric social relations – mediated by capital – involves fetishising processes. Social relations of power cannot be divorced from the dynamic of capital, as capitalism is a specific social relation. In this sense, socialisation implies crisis, contradiction but also objectification and reification.

Socialisation can be understood as an area traversed by forces, with the individual subjects that have will to power. That will to power is structured in certain universes. We are not talking about a simple aggregate of individuals but of intersubjective subjects, related as always in structures of power or institutions of more or less permanence. Each subject, as an actor, is an agent defined in relation to the others.

Adhering to the thread of our reflection, we can now affirm that certain places of socialisation for youth are fundamental: the clubs and bars of privilege, the malls and shopping centres of North American culture. Colonial logic rules and determines the interaction of subjects in these spaces. The answer is clear. Money is not enough. It is strictly required to follow a Western aesthetic model. At the 'prestigious' clubs we find the White youth or the *mestizo* whose colour of skin is not bronze. In this sense, the idea of race is always present in the socialisation of the periphery. Fernando Coronil writes: 'the idea of racial equality has been undermined by increasing segregation and discrimination, including what appear to be trivial incidents redefining racial frontiers – like the exclusion of people according to the colour of their skin from the discothèques of the high and middle classes' (2000: 97; original tranlation).

Besides belonging to a core of economic solvency, to be prestigious in the periphery requires first and foremost corporeal capital, and then the symbolic which enforces the image of the hegemonic colonial stereotype.

Following the logic imposed by capitalism in the era of globalisation, the malls have become a privileged space of socialisation among the countries of the periphery. It is here that the patterns of inclusion, exclusion and coloniality are neatly exposed.

Fashion, current cultural tendencies and the idea of novelty in general – concepts with an affinity to capitalism – dominate these spaces.

In the first half of the twentieth century, prior to the existence of shopping malls, Walter Benjamin (2002) caught a glimpse of the need to have merchandise to create a commercial space that would congregate a grand variety of products. Today, at the dawn of the twenty-first century, we can observe that at the malls big brand names, different commercial chains and imperial cultures coexist. The shopping malls are the temple of consumption and the merchandise is the new Golden Calf.

At the shopping malls, young people acquire prestige, the symbols of success. Clothing is one of these elements.[16] Fashion, as semiologist Roland Barthes (2003) observed, is a complex system. Each accessory is a sign or carrier text of information and meaning. The logo of the brand is a sign of status. Following this logic, Naomi Klein (2001) described how consumers of North America, when buying clothes, not only sought a garment to satisfy their needs but also looked for the company or designer signature as well; that is, they seek the prestige. We note, therefore, that for the consumer, the logo is everything.

Discursive practices are never neutral. In the case of the periphery, they normally respond to the patterns of coloniality, as it is the transnational corporations and commercial firms that occupy peripheral territories, as well as the illusions and misfortunes of the inhabitants. We should not forget, for example, that Shell was involved in the assassination of an Ogoni chief in Niger who opposed the company's operations; that Nike has dealings with Central American *maquiladoras* which exploit child labour and that Pepsi sponsored dictatorships in Nigeria (Klein, 2001).

The commercial centres represent places of colonisation, symbolic spaces oriented towards a certain type of consumption, given that the products and services that are offered there are intrinsically linked to the American Way of Life (Ritzer, 1999). The shopping mall is a space, as has been demonstrated, where multiple products coexist: food, video games, cinema, clothing, electronics, banks, internet cafes. Following Marx, we can say that the merchandise represents, above all, a particular type of social relation. These are explained, to be clear, as asymmetric social relations among actors or social classes as well as among the countries of the world. The social relations established in a club or in a shopping mall respond to the logic of the capitalist world economy (Wallerstein, 1991), basically designed by the transnational corporations, the true rectors of the world-system.

Internationally, colonial relations are established among countries, or more specifically, between colonisers and the colonised. The first colonisers and, more specifically, their *criollo* descendants – in the case of Latin America – establish an elite or ruling caste that tends towards reproducing the patterns of Western life. The superiority of this elite is founded on the idea of race: the White person is coloniser, Man; all other subjects with another colour of skin are inferior, savage, barbarian: the colonised. In Latin America we can observe that the *criollo* core is not only economically powerful but also enjoys a privileged place in the intellectual environment and holds much prestige in all activities of society. *Criollo* prestige is maintained and affirmed in opposition to the other racial strata: *mestizo*, Indigenous people or Black people.

This disdain for the colonised by the coloniser produces a particular way of understanding reality. The world *should be* as *it is* in the countries of the core. This slogan has been internalised among people of white – as among those of dark – skin. Groups of White people in the periphery experience an interesting state of being – the 'double consciousness' coined by Du Bois (1990); that is, the pain of not being European and the pride of not belonging to inferior races. Such a concept allows us to understand the coloniality of doing (Martínez Andrade, 2008).

In Mexico, we observe constant pejorative references to the *naco* or *cholito*. These expressions tell us different things. In the first place, it is an atrocious disdain for original peoples and popular culture. Second, *naco* is contrasted with colonial ideas of exquisiteness, elegance, ideas which, at the end of the day, are identified with the civilising process. Internal coloniality allows for the reproduction of patterns of domination, exploitation and control by some elites (racial, political, economic and cultural) over populations occupied territorially or culturally. The internalisation of discursive practices and ideologies promotes the repudiation of that which is culturally original or 'racially inferior'. In this sense, the *naco* or *cholo* is an individual that is linked to the physiognomy of original peoples or those who are distinguished by their popular habitus. Within colonial society, there exists a particular kind of apartheid; that is to say, a specific form of segregation based on somatic, economic and cultural characteristics.

A clear example of Latin American apartheid is the racial-economic segregation of social organisation. In general, foreigners and *criollos* reside in exclusive living quarters, have private health care and attend schools and universities of high status; meanwhile *mestizos* live in popular areas, have difficulty accessing social services and try to get some public help. It is important to recall here that it is the *criollos*, their children and the foreigners who attend the private schools of higher socio-economic standing. And so we follow Frantz Fanon, when he says: 'In the colonies the economic infrastructure is also a superstructure. The cause is effect: You are rich because you are white, you are white because you are rich' (2004: 5).

The liberation of the periphery is a condition *sine qua non*, politically as well as ethically, of another – equitable – world. Such liberation can be forged by cannibalising[17] (Campos, 2000) the discursive practices in the West; that is, by radically assimilating the rational modern core; but, as Eduardo Galeano pointed out a number of years ago: 'it is impossible to desire the end without desiring the means. Those who deny liberation to Latin America also deny our only possible rebirth, and incidentally absolve the existing structures from blame' (1997: 7).

Coloniality, the world-system and modernity, as hegemonic discourses, should be confronted and challenged critically at all planes of social reality. To capitulate in theoretical battles is to submit to the colonial precepts and paradigms. Social processes are mediated by power relations. Power, Foucault insisted, is not a metaphysical entity; rather it is an historically constructed social relation. By power we produce discourses, and we negate or exclude others. There are hegemonic and counter-hegemonic discourses. While hegemonic discourses are configured by social-individual practices which assure a continuum of the narrative, counter-hegemonic discourses provoke – in the Latin sense of the word, ruptures, subversions and explosions.

To acknowledge the presence of power structures does not imply disempowering the subject – in constant irruption within the standard myths of culture – with regard to his/her creative and transformative capacity. Rather, it is about recognising the mechanisms of control which impede the emergence of other voices, other points of view, other discourses and other social practices. The logic of hegemonic discourse is intrinsically linked to a dynamic of control, domination and specified exploitation. Its ontological, cultural or epistemic *telos* is marked geopolitically by a structural inequality imposed at the dawn of the sixteenth century.

The fall of 'actually existing socialism' reinforced the impunity of the countries of the core, led principally by the USA, and consolidated a new economic doctrine (neoliberalism), forging a political entelechy (representative, liberal democracy) of the hegemonic narrative. In this panorama, the imperial organisms (World Bank, International Monetary Fund, World Trade Organisation, etc.) the multinational corporations

(McDonald's, Nike, Ford, among others) and the countries of the core (G8) merge as neurological centres of power. The *humiliatocracy* (*edhalloukratia*) is a form of governance by dominating classes. Power relations are not only materialised in individual or collective habitus or practices, but in signs and discourse objects as well. It is for this reason that we turn our interest towards a critical analysis of the imperial symbol: the shopping mall or commercial centre.

Conclusion

The shopping mall is a central object of discourse in the hegemonic colonial narrative, given that, on the one hand, it is an important element of the symbolic configuration of the social imaginary. On the other hand, it consolidates the influence of transnational capital in the everyday life of its people. Consumer society gives us a basic ideal in a developed, democratic and – most of all – civilised world.

Social subjects are not a *tabula rasa*; rather, they emerge from a complex accumulation of situations and events, and – as Bourdieu would point out – an incorporated history. The relevance of the concept of habitus lies in demonstrating the material-subjective conditions and their influence, in the doing of agents. Going beyond the visions of revisionist and other reductionists, we think that the contributions of Foucault and Bourdieu allow us to recognise the transcendence of power structures in the social imaginary.

It is essential to state here that we are not attempting to explain the Latin American experience through social theories that are so far removed from our material reality. On the contrary, we attempt to contextualise geopolitically the analytical tools (concepts and categories) that reveal and unravel the mechanisms of control, power and domination of hegemonic discourses. For these we refer to the theoretical contributions of such thinkers as Frantz Fanon, Enrique Dussel, Aníbal Quijano, among others, to go beyond Eurocentric perspectives. Latin America needs to recognise its cultural dependency and colonial atavisms in order to unleash a struggle of liberation in all aspects (gnoseological, ethical, political-economic and aesthetic, etc.), and to find in this way a true ontological status. For this, we need to be conscious of our material-subjective situation. That is, understanding our coloniality would give us coherence in our locus of enunciation. The victim's pain is not abstract, it is the fruit of a praxis of concrete domination.

We maintain that to think beyond liberation is to break with the hegemonic paradigm and to really recognise other worldviews (*Weltanschauungen*), other practices and other discourses; not as an act of condescending abasement (*kenosis*) 'giving the word', as proposed by some prideful perspectives; rather, as an asymmetric dialogue among peoples.

Part Two

Utopia and Liberation

3

The Portentous Eclosion of the Principle of Hope:[1] Ernst Bloch and Liberation

In the 56-page report on the United Nations (UN) Millennium Development Goals (United Nations, 2009) we can find the most despicable features of the economic system. The officials and bureaucrats of the main international financial institutions (the World Trade Organization, International Monetary Fund and World Bank, among others) boast of the 'humanitarian aid' dispensed over recent years. However, the good intentions of eradicating poverty in 2015 have vanished in the face of a reality where 1.02 billion people suffer from hunger daily.[2] According to the report, 51 per cent of the Sub-Saharan population appeared to be living on US\$ 1.25 per day, while emissions of carbon dioxide worldwide reached 28.275 billion metric tons. Furthermore, deforestation sweeps across 13 million hectares per year, an area approximately the size of Bangladesh. In short, the relation between poverty and environmental degradation is evident. In the prologue to the 2009 report, the Secretary-General of the UN, Ban Ki-Moon, recognises that: 'The timing is ripe for making the structural changes that are needed to move more decisively towards more equitable development and sustainability and to address the climate crisis' (United Nations, 2009: 3).

For his part, the Mexican Secretary of Social Development, Ernesto Cordero in 2009, challenged the figures presented by the World Bank, stating that in his country 14 million people live on less than US\$ 2.50 per day and 40 million on less than US\$ 4.50 per day.[3] The National Council of Social Policy Evaluation (CONEVAL) revealed that between 2006 and 2008, the number of people who did not meet the required daily caloric intake rose from 14.4 to 19.5 million.[4]

In *The principle of hope*[5] we read: 'Very little, all too little has been said so far about hunger' (Bloch I, 1996: 65). Hunger, an ontic and ontological concern, deserves to be approached from a perspective contrary to the positions assumed by reformists and neo-institutionalists of the hegemonic system. And so we shall attempt to analyse the pertinence of concrete utopia in the construction of counter-hegemonic alternatives through the contributions of German philosopher Ernst Bloch. Our objective is, in the first instance, to observe the concern with hunger and the abstraction of nature in the 'encyclopaedia of utopias',[6] that is, *The principle of hope*. Second, we shall try to follow its influence on the theology and philosophy of liberation exposed by Leonardo Boff and Enrique Dussel, who have manifested their sympathies with Bloch's work.

We agree with the affirmation provided by Francisco Serra, who in his preface to the Spanish-language version of *The principle of hope* (Bloch I: 18) suggests: 'one never finishes reading Bloch, because he has become a classic and he has discovered a scantly explored territory, the territory of hope; but in order to make sense, hope should be mediated, founded and contrasted with a reality that always finds itself resisting change'. Therefore, it is imperative to embark upon a politically interested re-reading of Bloch's work with the purpose of confronting the fetishised truths of power. The winds of time demand it. Our peoples require it.

The Principle of Hope and the Utopic Function

The principle of hope undoubtedly represents a major contribution to political thought and philosophy. This text, which was written between 1938 and 1947, and, more importantly, worked on and edited in the United States and Germany, is one of the most valued showcases of thought on utopic thinking. A German Jew and an atheist by conviction, Ernst Bloch, was a student of George Simmel and Max Weber. Between 1912 and 1914 he participated in the study circle headed by Max Weber, a group which also saw the participation of such figures as Ferdinand Tönnies, Werner Sombart, Ernst Troeltsch, Paul Honigsheim[7] and George Lukács. Eva Karadi (1986: 69–70) relates that Bloch and Lukács arrived in the city of Heidelberg in May 1912, with the idea of developing themselves and with wanting to participate in the intellectual production of the time. The meetings of the Heidelberg circle took place on Sunday mornings at Weber's house, located on Ziegelhäuser Street. With time, however, the two friends came to a parting of the ways in their eschatological ideas of the world and their pragmatic political strategies. In an excellent article, Miguel Vedda (2007: 97) analyses the ontological and philosophical controversies between Bloch and the young Lukács, and reveals how, ironically, Lukács passage to Marxism only made such differences more acute.

Empty Hands

The opening words of *The principle of hope* are interesting, as Bloch exposes here the relationship between anguish and existence, themes which run throughout the entire work. 'I move. From early on we are searching. All we do is crave, cry out. We do not have what we want' (Bloch, 1996: 21). Anguish,[8] as an expression of the incomplete realisation of the human being is treated by Bloch from psychological,[9] ontological[10] and social[11] perspectives. Actually, one of his disciples, the German-French philosopher Arno Münster (2007: 159) emphasises the dialectical relation that Bloch establishes between hope and anguish, to demonstrate that the hope Bloch endorses is not in any sense abstract or without a philosophy of praxis (*sub specie utopiae*) or *docta spes*.

'Foundations', part two of *The principle of hope*, consists of 14 chapters that outline the pillars of 'utopic function'. Undoubtedly, we highlight the impulse or *suum esse conservare* (self-preservation) of a living corporeality,[12] that is, the manifestation par excellence of the will to live;[13] the appetite of the affects of active hope (Bloch I, 1996: 70) and the distinction between nocturnal dreams and conscious dreams. From all this we should consider that the drive leads us to a 'future horizon' represented in the archetype of *summum bonum*, since humans paint their wishful images through different cultural manifestations: art, social utopias, religions, etc.

The human being always seeks a way to survive in this world. The human being tries, through diverse methods, to satisfy his/her physical, ludic, material and ontological needs.[14] Nevertheless, in being a socio-historical subject, the human being is mediated by desires, projections and specific concerns and, therefore, the context should not be circumvented:

> In short, all definitions of basic drives only flourish in the soil of their own time and are limited to that time. For this reason they cannot be made absolute, even less separated from the economic being of mankind in each age. (Bloch, 1996: 69)

As we can observe, Bloch reclaims the notion of *form*[15] to comprehend the production of human 'images of hope'. In this sense, and distancing ourselves from the postmodern current, we are conscious that material conditions shape certain aspects of the cultural or political logic of a society (Žižek, 2001).

Hunger, as the source for the drive forwards (Bloch I, 1996: 75) or *horror vacui* is comprised not only in the intersubjective configuration of human beings but serves also as an element in popular emancipation. As was once written, in September 1911, by a man committed to liberation: 'the government has not understood that you rebel because you hunger' (Flores, 1993: 50). Hunger, 'the leading force of production' (Bloch I: 361), mobilises subjects and, at the same time, makes sense of the images of hope that inspire processes of change, leading to the inseparable union of danger and faith.

> The No to the bad situation which exists, the Yes to the better life that hovers ahead, is incorporated by the deprived into revolutionary interest. This interest always begins with hunger, hunger transforms itself, having been taught, into an explosive force against the prison of deprivation. (Bloch, 1996: 75)

The 'appetite of the expectant emotions' (Bloch, 1996: 70) brings us to the eschatological sphere of hope[16] and, therefore, to religion – as an analytical space, where tensions and 'elective affinities' are expressed among worldviews participating in the social configuration.[17] 'Active hope', as a messianic element, constitutes a guiding attitude and half-open door to the 'horizons of the future', characterising the utopias of subjects.[18]

Ernst Bloch differentiates between abstract utopia and concrete utopia.[19] For him, the first is expressed in political projects of bourgeois roots (fascism or national-socialism, for example), and in the neutral abstractions of a-historic aesthetics, images of hope which decorate the deception of capitalist ideology (Bloch I: 40). The second is a hatching[20] in the social framework, a concrete political project of social emancipation that goes forward – a concrete abstraction of revolutionary reason. Chapter 14 is axial as it is here that Bloch establishes the distinction between dreams at night and conscious dreams.

Through this oneiric language, the subconscious works the repressed elements through the ego and, in this sense, Bloch (I: 90) identifies three characteristics in dreams of night: (1) censorship is non-existent; (2) the presence of daily residues or disconnected representations and (3) the impossibility of praxis. It should also be stated here that in night dreams satisfaction of desires or representations of anguish (*pavor nocturnus*) are realised. Although on many occasions conscious dreams can end up in escapist images,[21] their potential lies in that all the subject's forces can be channelled towards transforming the world; in day dreams we can paint a better world. It is worth mentioning that Bloch is inspired by contributions from psychoanalysis and analytical psychology which treats the subconscious and the function of dreams. However, he emphasises:

> And most importantly: the respective psychoanalytical basic drives that are emphasised are not basic drives at all in the strict sense, they are too partial. They do not break through so unequivocally as say – hunger, the drive that is *always left out of psychoanalytical theory*; they are not such final authorities as the simple drive to keep oneself alive. This drive is the self-preservation drive, it alone might be so fundamental – no matter what changes occur – as to set all the other drives in motion in the first place. (Bloch, 1996: 64)

On the other hand, Bloch argues that conscious dreams are intrinsically linked to the aesthetic sphere because they are responsible for artistic pre-appearance. For Heinz Kimmerle (1986: 210), pre-appearance (*Vor-schein*) clarifies the search that is not-yet-realised, in the political and cultural sense as the expression not-yet-realised, which is the not-yet-attained.

Concrete Tendency of the Humanisation of Nature

Not only does capitalism break down social links but it systematically destroys the environment as well. The process of abstraction and subsumption of labour converts human beings and nature into simple instruments for the production of commercial goods. Capital is the negation of life in the broadest sense of the word. In this respect, Marx (2007: 423) was convinced that the process implied martyrdom for the producer and in this sense all 'progress' and the art of robbing the worker implies the art of stealing from the Earth. In short, the capitalist system – understood not only as a mode of production but as a specific social relation as well – is reified by annihilating the two sources of all wealth: Earth and Man.

In *Capital contre nature*, Michael Löwy (2003: 21) suggests that the ecological question is a great challenge for the renovation of Marxist thought in the twenty-first century, as it implies a radial break with the idea of linear progress, and the economic and technological paradigm of modern industrial civilisation. It is here that our reflection is inscribed, in pondering the contributions of Ernst Bloch (I: 247) in relation to 'humanising nature'. In the terrain of political ecology we consider that *The principle of hope* possesses very significant theoretical elements which continue to be indispensable for a critique of the capitalist system. To scrutinise the subversive utopic core, Bloch's proposal can be put to good use in the recomposition of the oppositional horizon.

The critique elaborated by Hans Jonas (2005: 370), someone who called Bloch the 'glorious *enfant terrible* of utopism', is based primarily on the notion that his not-yet does not allow him to observe what is now. Perhaps the discordance lies in the different concepts of Nature. Whereas Bloch values the almost inexhaustible creative potential of production in the alliance between man and nature, inscribed in a concrete utopia (optimist-humanist and neo-Marxist), Jonas holds a realist-pessimist view influenced by gnostic philosophy and apocalyptic pessimism.

For his part, the philosopher Arno Münster (2010: 54) destroys the false interpretations, that is, those that turn Bloch into an apologist for utopias or, worse yet, identifying his work with the praise of dictatorships. Münster recalls that, since 1956, Ernst Bloch criticised the Soviet model, as the latter always stood for a '*novum humanum*' founded upon a true democracy. And for our part, it is a theoretical-practical imperative to ponder his approach to eco-politics given that, despite the ideological bombardment of the 'end of history' or the supposed de-legitimising of revolution offered by postmodern and neoliberal currents, concrete utopias and eco-socialism today are essential. Bloch is, therefore, a touchstone for contemporary critical thinking.[22]

In the analysis of the concrete tendency of *natura naturans* or *supernaturans* – in Bloch's terms – we focus on four axes of the encyclopaedia of utopias, because we believe that they are necessary in the construction of an eco-political project that struggles for the liberation of humankind and nature.[23] These axes are: (1) a critique of bourgeois society, (2) Francis Bacon's philosophical claim of *regnum hominis*, (3) the *unio mystica* as a shared experience between nature and religion and, finally, (4) the concrete technique necessary in order to critically assimilate *The principle of hope* into an eco-socialist project.

Natura Dominata

Capitalist social relations are underpinned in abstraction. In the process of making value, the producer is alienated while nature is objectified, producing – as Löwy (2003: 15) remarks – a rupture between the metabolism (*Riss des Stofwechels*) of societies and nature. Following Marx, James O'Connor (1998) comments that capitalism hosts the immanent contradictions between capital and labour on the one hand, and the forces of production versus natural conditions for production on the other; that is, nature *tout court*.

In its predatory logic, capitalism objectifies the human being and nature for the sake of creating surplus value. Environmental destruction took a turn during the European Industrial Revolution, given that it implied not only the rise of a mentality based on abstract ideas (progress, unlimited growth and linear development) but also contributed to the mechanisation[24] of humankind–nature, resulting in the promotion of technological messianism at the terrible cost of harm to the eco-system.

In the analysis of the fetishised form of bourgeois society it is essential to return to Marx,[25] given that his critique revealed material, subjective and ideological mechanisms which operate in the hegemonic system. Marxism, as humanity in action, does not remain stuck within the boundaries of theory; rather, it supposes a radical transformation of society, that is, wanting something that needs to be done (Bloch III: 485). Consequently, sobriety and enthusiasm continue to be two sides of the same coin for social emancipation:

> In the former case, by human beings becoming masters of their own socialisation, i.e. mediated with themselves as the producing subject of history; in the latter case, by increasing mediation taking place with the previously obscure production and conditional basis of the laws of nature. (Bloch, 1996: 698)

In the process of production capital absorbs 'living labour', converting the worker into an object. However, the process of objectification is not only material, but ideological as well. The symbolic structures – such as language and imaginaries – express the system's dynamic. For this reason Bloch, following Marx, always emphasised the abstract character of the word 'humanity', as the human being has to be conceived as the 'host of social relations'; contrary to the axiological idea of bourgeois humanism, it claims the pathos of practical activity. In other words, for Marx as well as for Bloch, it is only in the praxis of liberation that the human being achieves real victory over self-alienation.

Regnum Hominis

Francis Bacon's famous phrase 'knowledge is power' has been the object of harsh criticism by sociologists (Santos, 2002) as well as philosophers (Jonas, 2005) and theologists (Boff, 1993) of various schools of thought, as for some it justifies domination and encourages environmental degradation. Without going deeply into these issues and contributing to the allegations, we find it interesting that Bloch claims this *ars inveniendi* provided by Bacon.

Raimundo Lulio 'the curious scholastic rationalist', as Bloch (II: 20) would call him, influenced not only Giordano Bruno, Pico della Mirandola, Pascal and Leibniz but also Francis Bacon. In the writings of this last we can appreciate the intention of getting to a 'fundamental form' of things and, most of all, the phenomenal self-application of the experiment. For Bloch (II: 232), the goal of knowing was for the English planner not knowledge for knowledge's sake; rather it was the empowerment of knowledge, the creation of a new Atlantis where all is at the service of humankind. From there, *Novum organon* coincides with a higher alchemy identified with the dream of Joaquín de Fiore. In this sense, Bloch identifies *The great restoration* as an update of old tales and the intention to approach that which is found beyond the pillars of Hercules.

Nova Atlantis – even with its technical optimism – is understood by Bloch (II: 236) as an outline of *regnum hominis*, stating that:

> Admittedly the contact with nature remained in the bourgeois economy and society which arrived, but it remained sufficiently abstract and unmediated. Bacon's great maxim: '*Natura parendo vincitur*', nature is conquered by obedience, remained active, but it was crossed by the interest of an 'exploitation' of nature, and this by an interest which has nothing more to do with *natura naturans* which Bacon still knows and singles out as the *causa causarum* let alone being allied to it.

As we can observe, Bloch demarks certain responsibilities of Bacon's legacy, suggesting another reading of the *oeuvre*.

Unio Mystica

Bloch (I: 45) constantly accentuated the fabulous features of nature. All through 'the encyclopaedia of utopias', we find references to the clouds, the sea and the starry skies,[26] water, landscapes, gardens, the Arcadia, etc. For him, the *priority* of nature is manifested in the elaborations of images of hope, as the utopic Totum[27] – embodied in the terrain of the aesthetic and mystic – has no end. By mystic, following Leonardo Boff and Frei Betto (1999: 21), we mean the set of deep convictions and passions that mobilise people and movements in their desire for change, while at the same time inspiring practices and actions intended to confront any type of difficulties or obstacles, sustaining hope in the face of historical defeats. In that respect, Bloch rescues the sense of pastoral vision found in religious attitudes, in order to contemplate the search for the yet-to-be: the homeland (*La Patria*). It is no coincidence that Bloch reclaims the notion of *cosmic community* from the Stoic Cleanthes (Bloch II: 55), the pertinence of the *vita activa–vita contemplativa* of the Franciscan rule (Bloch III: 39), the Taoist *wu yu wu wie* (Bloch III: 343), and even in considering Gaia (Bloch II: 381): 'for Earth is an unfinished space of a theatrical scene that has not yet been written'. Nor does Bloch's influence on Boff surprise us.[28]

The notion of *unio mystica* is religious as it refers to the 'anti-trivial' sphere (Bloch III: 408). Löwy states that religion occupies a privileged place within the immense cartography of utopic landscapes espoused by Bloch, and in this sense reference to the mystical does not escape his theoretical reflections.

Natural elements are also present in the rites, myths and liturgies of the religious imaginary. The turn to the elements of nature in religion is fundamental to the construction of its traditions and in the consolidation of its place of memory. For this reason Dussel (1977: 83) points out that water, as a universal element of life, reminds us of our relation to nature, it is found in plants and animals. In baptism we bow to the purifying power of water and nature; water is the matter of equality and natural liberty.

It is worth stating here that the relation to nature may vary; the pantheist might look differently towards interaction with nature than the Christian, who will act according to their ethical-mythical notions. Nevertheless, *deep ecology* has accused Christianity of being the main culprit in environmental degradation (Filoramo, 1993). For us, although the theological myths and interpretations play an important role with regard to nature, this role cannot be de-contextualised from the socio-economic dynamic. In other words, 'the gods of death' can teleologically pervert the ethical-mythical core and realise the sacrifice of victims; but throughout the tempests of history, a prophet always arises: he who subverts religion and announces the Gospel, shows us the way towards liberation!

Concrete Technique

According to Pierre Furlan (1986: 201), Bloch, in chapter 37 of *The principle of hope*, develops a critique of technical reason that is, in the end, a critique of modern alienation. For Furlan, it suffices to say that the mode of appropriation of resources – on behalf of capitalism – has been realised under the barrel of a gun, converting nature into a wasteland. We believe that it is necessary to add two more considerations to this critique: (1) the distinction between abstract calculation and concrete abstraction, and (2) the difference between abstract technique and concrete technique.

By bourgeois abstract calculation, Bloch visualises a fetishised attitude provoked by the capitalist ethos, consisting of accumulation per se, the madness of quantification, the obsession with growth, the values of *homo economicus*. Opposed to this *logos*, we understand 'concrete abstraction' to be an intellectual activity that looks at the human being as an end and not the means. The horizon ahead of the *regnum hominis* is, therefore, the liberating *ratio* that rises against bourgeois instrumental reasoning.

Hans Jonas (2005) criticised the supposed 'technological messianism' in Bloch. But this accusation is unfounded, as Bloch always recognised that technique was never neutral and therefore its usefulness responds to the societal norm.[29] In this sense, abstract technique serves to perfect exploitation of nature and humankind. Enrique Dussel (2003) calls on Jonas's erroneous ontological claim, given that he started off by treating being without taking into consideration concrete reality. Jonas's suspicion of Marxism brought him to a naïve path of critique without having considered specific social relations. The concrete technique contributes to mediation among human beings and between human beings and nature. It facilitates the production of subsistent material conditions that ultimately set the framework for social reproduction.

According to the most concrete of all Marx's anticipations, the essence of the perfectible is 'the naturalisation of man, the humanisation of nature'. That is the abolition of alienation in man and nature, between man and nature or the harmony of the un-reified object with the manifested subject, of the un-reified subject with the manifested object. (Bloch, 1996: 240)

We are therefore convinced that the portentous eclosion of *The principle of hope* lies in articulating the most perverse effects of capital: the ominous situation of miserable and terrible ecocide. We argue that eco-socialism, as a concrete utopia should push for social emancipation and liberation of the planet. To delink the social and political struggles from environmental problems is to commit a fatal error. Earth should be liberated and the whip of Man should be eliminated.

Oskar Negt (2007: 47) reclaims the idea of 'walking righteously' as the base of all authentic revolutions, as dignity plays an important role in the process of emancipation. For Negt, the hope that Bloch proposes is a category which belongs to politics rather than to traditional philosophy because it is one that speaks to emancipation. That is, in contrast to thinkers who are intent on reducing Bloch's hope to a kind of wishful thinking, Bloch himself always recognised the contingent character of the social dynamic, *ergo* its tendencies and latencies.

Nothing which appears in nature and in society is assured and guaranteed, much less progress and humanity ... History looks more like an accumulation of ruins and destroyed, dispersed and broken hopes, than a logic of organised progress following the stages to be overcome. Bloch's theme is not that of the victors but that of the defeated, the oppressed, the humiliated and the violated, who nonetheless engender signs that, generally speaking, can no longer be erased from the collective memory of mankind. (Negt, 2007: 49)

Cur Deus Homo

In contrast to many thinkers who reduce religion to a simple process of human alienation, constricting its meaning to the term 'opium', Ernst Bloch parts from this atavism and identifies the presence of the utopic-revolutionary Totum woven into the lines of faith[30] of many cultures. For Michèle Bertrand (1986: 185), belief is a subjective fact (*fait subjectif*). Its origin is not simply psychological but of the social order and, therefore, belief as a social phenomenon is contradictory; it escapes neither the antagonistic dynamic nor the explosive logic of culture.

The religious dimension in *The principle of hope* is analysed in two ways: (a) as a producer of images of hope that consolidate alienation and (b) as a redeeming latency which mobilises people against worldly misery. Belief as subversion is one of Bloch's cardinal points, as it gains political meaning, *sursum corda*, in the impulse to make the world a better place.[31] The phrase 'we raise our hearts' is mediated by a messianic substrate where religion as 'desirous essence' (Bloch III: 313) is utopic in itself. Michael Löwy (2005b: 51) infers that for Bloch, what is innovative and meaningful in the messianic and prophetic is that, in contrast to contemporary religions, destiny can be changed. While the Moira in the Hellenic world, or the astral myths of the ancient Egyptians, presuppose an irrevocable destiny leading to quietism and powerlessness, Judaic prophesy conceives destiny as a balance where it is precisely the human being that is the decisive factor. Counter-posing pessimism and the desperateness of Cassandra or the fatalism of the Greek oracle, the prophet Isaiah proves that destiny is not categorical, rather it is hypothetical, given that it is dependent on morals and the free will of human beings (Bloch III: 45).

The religious aspect constitutes one of the main pillars of *The principle of hope* and is found, undoubtedly, in chapter 53 where Bloch makes explicit the utopic function and the ambivalence of religion. Ambivalent in the sense that religion can ideologically or politically reinforce a system of oppression or, on the contrary, religion can serve as a critical discourse on such domination. In the first sense, Bloch (III: 335) says that it is in abstract utopias that images of hope are bred into alienating religion – that is, in an a-historic delirium. In relation to the second sense – religion as subversion – Bloch insists on the importance of the critical-explosive content in the construction of emancipatory practices.[32] Religion can therefore not be read exclusively as opium (Bloch III: 209).

The kernel of the question elaborated by Hegel as well as Feuerbach is Saint Anslemo's *Cur Deus homo?* (Why did God become man?), interpreted by Bloch (III: 408) as the process of 'anthropologisation' of religion, where the concept of Man is projected in a utopic figure (*homo absconditus*), or incomplete man. Needless to say, Bloch distances himself from Feuerbach's mechanical-materialist nature and his bourgeois notion of Man, considering it too narrow; although Bloch credits him with disenchanting heaven in order to make Man important.[33]

The Principle of Liberation or the Cry for Emancipation

During the 1970s, Latin America experienced the imposition of an economic, political and cultural model which strengthened the trasnational corporations; this imposition was realised with the undeniable help of the US government and Latin American military juntas, as the 1969 Rockefeller Report on America corroborates (Cockcroft, 2001). Those years are key in understanding the real configuration of the world-system and the critical *locus* of the liberationist proposals coming from the periphery. It marks the beginning of the Kondratieff phase B, which Wallerstein called the end of the 'Glorious Thirty'.[34] By way of research under the direction of Donella and Dennis Meadows in 1972, the Club of Rome recognised the limits of growth and, between 1970 and 1980 Latin America increased its external debt from US\$ 27 billion to US\$ 231 billion, which implied the annual payment of US\$ 18 billion in interest. The hideous debt is the result of an established relationship between the North Atlantic and heinous military dictatorships. Prophetically, the theology and philosophy of liberation sprang forth in this context, as expressions of a 'Christianity of Liberation' (Löwy, 1998) which confronted the gods of death, the idols of capital and barbarism.

Bloch's work did not go unnoticed by Latin American theologians and philosophers of liberation. Michael Löwy (2005b: 53) tells us that it is no surprise that Bloch became one of the main sources of inspiration for Gustavo Gutiérrez, the Peruvian founder of liberation theology. For our part, we propose an analysis of the repercussions that *The principle of hope* had on the works of Brazilian theologian Leonardo Boff and the Argentine philosopher Enrique Dussel, in order to detect the possible eclosions of the utopian function in relation to the humanisation of nature.

Luis Gerardo Nuñez Díaz (2009: 205) claims that Latin America has been a fertile ground for utopic reflection. For this reason he took it upon himself to track the critical force of hope in the theological proposals of the liberationists. Just as *The principle of hope* contributed to the architecture of the theology of hope (Jürgen Moltmann), the same work reinforced the arguments of liberation theology.

Theology and Bio-civilisation

In 1972, Brazilian liberation theologian Leonardo Boff published his *Jesus Christ liberator*, making important contributions to the political-religious culture of liberationist Christianity. Although the book makes scant reference to Marxism, it does highlight Ernst Bloch's work. Since the 1970s, Leonardo Boff (1972: 58) has highlighted the importance of utopic elements[35] in the elaboration of a Christology for Latin America. Providing arguments against the idea that reduces utopia to a simple evasion of reality, Boff assumes the critical potential of utopic thought.

Leonardo Boff is one of the liberation theologists who has done the most work on ecological aspects of reality. His book *Ecologia, mundalização, espiritualidade* was published one year after the Rio Summit in 1992, and Boff confesses that it was his Franciscan education that made him sensitive to ecological questions (Tamayo, 1999). For the Brazilian theologian, the primary victims of the current model are the poor and Earth crucified (Boff, 2008a: 68). The fact that 79 per cent of humanity lives in the poor global South, and that every year the number of people living in slums or vulnerable zones increases, cannot be ignored. Unfortunately, in the face of this situation, solidarity is reduced as the majority of rich countries do not use even 0.7 per cent of their gross national product to help out the countries of the poor, as recommended by the UN.[36] Extreme poverty and environmental degradation are the result of an economic and political system that is clearly defined as capitalism.

In *Ecologia: grito da terra, grito dos pobres* (2004a), Leonardo Boff recuperates the use of the ontological phrase 'Cry' – the cry of human suffering provoked by an economic, socio-political and cultural system that seeks to maintain the consolidation of capitalism. In this very work, Boff pushes for convergence between the Principle of Responsibility and the Principle of Hope, while considering necessary a radical change in our civilisational paradigm. From this we consider his approach to deep ecology but assimilate it critically to rethink ethical-ecological and social questions.

For Leonardo Boff (2009: 50) it is of the utmost importance to construct a planetary civilisation which holds Earth as the centre. This bio-civilisation (*biocivilização*) should be based on five pillars: (1) sustainable, responsible and harmonious use of limited natural resources and services; (2) the value of the use of goods should have primacy over their commercial value; (3) democratic control should be constructed upon social relations; (4) the minimal world ethos should come as a result of multicultural exchange, emphasising the ethics of care, compassion, cooperation and universal responsibility; and, finally, (5) spirituality, as an expression of human unity and not as a monopoly of religion.

Sociologist Lucien Goldmann (1976: 15) interprets worldview (*Weltanschauung*) to be: 'not an immediate, empirical fact, but a conceptual working hypothesis indispensable to an understanding of the way in which individuals actually express their ideas'. While its expression transcends the work or thought of an author, its importance lies in demonstrating that human deeds constitute significant global structures. Goldmann recognises the significance of Dilthey's reflections in the elaboration of this analytical tool but argues that, unfortunately, Dilthey did not give it a 'positive and rigorous' status. For our part, we believe that one of Goldmann's contributions was his revealing of world vision[37] and the dynamics of social classes.[38] The study and analysis of a writer's work cannot be divorced from their biographical antecedents or background, nor from their ideological positions.

It is worth stating here that the concept 'world vision', as a group of aspirations, feelings and ideas which unite a certain group (social class) or opposes other groups, is fundamental in understanding struggles and conflicts, not only at the social level but also in the area of social theory. For Lucien Goldmann (1976) all worldviews have a functional character in relation to privileged social groups, and therefore the worldview is presented as a means to help those groups in managing the problems that lie before them, at the service of other groups and nature. However, as Goldmann himself has indicated, it is not simply about making reference to supposed influences; rather, the point is to explain them. For this reason, and for the purposes of presenting an argument on the presence of *The principle of hope* or the influence that Bloch had on the musings of liberation theologists, we must first consider three structural elements of social life: (1) the particular importance of economic life; (2) the predominant historical function of social classes; and (3) the notion of possible consciousness. In this sense, being confined in a defined area (eschatological and socio-historical), the theologists of liberation had to base themselves on Marxist contributions in order to understand the social logic. The importance of Marxist social theory has been espoused in many works and, therefore, the approach to such a heretic thinker as Ernst Bloch was fundamental to understanding religion's critical and revolutionary drive.

Michael Löwy (2008: 13) identifies two world visions: one based on ideological visions when serving to legitimise, justify, defend or maintain the world social order and, another based on utopic visions,[39] which comply with the critical, negative, subversive function when searching for that non-existing reality. Löwy argues that ideology and utopia are two expressions of the same phenomena, that which Karl Mannheim called 'total ideology'. Löwy states that we should take seriously the term 'social world vision' when referring to the structured host of values, representations, ideas, images or cognitive orientations. Utopic social visions play a critical and negative role in the construction of a non-existent, yet-to-be reality.[40]

Son of Italian immigrants, Leonardo Boff was born in Concordia in 1938 and read philosophy and theology at Curitiba and Petropolis. In 1965 he was ordained as a priest in the Franciscan order.[41] Under Leo Scheffczyk, he completed his doctorate in theology at Munich, with a dissertation entitled *Die Kirche als Sakrament im Horizont der Welterfahung* (The Church as Sacrament). (It might be interesting to note that Joseph Ratzinger was a member of Boff's thesis examination committee.) Thereafter, he returned to Brazil in 1970.

As noted earlier, the 1970s was for Latin America a decade of repression and Brazil was no exception. The political commitment of some clergy has been documented.[42] In the case of Leonardo Boff, his pastoral activities were found in the framework of military repression and social unrest – due to the poverty and exclusion faced by the majority of Brazilians. At Petropolis, Rio de Janerio, Leonardo Boff began pastoral militancy on behalf of the poplar classes: *meninos das favelas y moradores da rua.*[43]

Petropolis is a city ridden with seismic problems, making it vulnerable to collapses. The earthquake of 1988 caused irreparable damage to many homes. For this reason, housing became one of the main programmes of the Centre for the Defence of Human Rights (CDDH).[44] Among its services, CDDH of Petropolis develops programmes of juridical and psychological help for victims of domestic violence, and promotes artistic activities among disadvantaged youth.

Leonardo Boff's contributions can also be appreciated in Brazil's landless peasant movement Movimento dos Trabalhadores Rurais Sem Terre (MST),[45] as the ex-Franciscan has openly expressed his support for this group. The preferential option for the poor continues to be the exegetical locus; Boff, however, incorporates the idea of the Earth as also being a victim of the system.[46]

Both texts, *Ecologia: grito da terra, grito dos pobres* and *Ecologia, mundialização, espiritualidade*, were written during the 1990s, coinciding with the Rio Earth Summit of 1992 in Rio and the definite fall of actually existing socialism in Eastern Europe. Much of his Franciscan career was dedicated to rescuing the contributions of such figures as Duns Scotus, Buenaventura (St Bonaventure) and Teilhard de Chardin.[47]

Leonardo Boff considers it fundamental to articulate the Principle of Responsibility, as elaborated by Han Jonas (2005: 40), who advocated working in such a way that one's actions should be compatible with the permanence of authentic human life on Earth. This is in harmony with Ernst Bloch's Principle of Hope, which looks towards the future, and the Principle of Care, which refers to the principle of compassion found in all great spiritual traditions of humanity East and West. For Boff, what is decisive is not religions but the spirituality that lies within them. The Principle of Care is thus holistic, spiritual and ecological; it proposes an alternative to materialist realism and aims at rescuing a sense of family for humanity. Among the characters identified by Boff as beings of care are: Jesus, Francis of Assisi (universal fraternity), Mother Teresa of Calcutta (principle of mercy) and Mahatma Ghandi (politics as care of the people). In overcoming Eurocentrism, Boff makes a critique of the asymmetrical structure of power between the centre and the periphery, and the ecocidal character of the capitalist system. In this sense, the liberation of the wretched of the Earth is intrinsically linked to Gaia.

> The utopic dream in this phase consists of the search for humanising the human being, challenged to live, beginning with his/her uniqueness, as a communitarian being, a being of cooperation, an ethical and spiritual being who takes responsibility for his/her actions so that these can be beneficial to all. This utopia should be concretised within the inevitable contradictions found in all historical processes and conflicts of interest. But it will mean a new horizon for hope that will nurture Humanity's journey towards the future. (Boff, 2006: 39)

The work that CDDH Petropolis[48] has been doing for years now, supported by Leonardo Boff, is significant to us, especially in the areas of raising awareness and civic education. Boff's praxis does not distance itself from the needs of those victims of actually existing modernity.

Leonardo Boff not only exalts the idea of social movements, he has been directly involved with them. For him, citizen power is constituted from below, from free associations, cooperatives and trade unions, etc. In this sense, for Boff, there is not one revolutionary vanguard in the strict Leninist sense. Rather, there is a historical bloc which contributes to disputing hegemony[49] and pressuring governments towards popular interests.

Politics, as a space of conflicts is not exempt from the external influences of economic, cultural or religious groups. Thus, civic education is necessary. The role of such social movements as the MST or the Unemployed Workers movement (Trabalhadores Desempregados) is paramount, given that, in this way, a sector of the 'people' becomes a political actor. The people for itself.

Additionally, Leonardo Boff (2006: 97) proposes the creation of a 'florestania'; that is, a citizenship of the forest. In the development paradigm, deforestation was synonymous with progress and under this logic deforestation takes place at a rate of 15 hectares per minute. It is no wonder, then, that at the 2009 World Social Forum, held in Belem, one of the main themes discussed was the deforestation of the Amazon basin and the growth of carbon dioxide emissions. At said forum, Leonardo Boff, Frei Betto and Michael Löwy were present; they reflected on and discussed eco-socialism.

For Boff, governments should and must respond to popular demands, since it is among the people or in the community that sovereignty lies. When government uses the state apparatus as an instrument to safeguard the interests of elites, the relationship between governors and governed becomes corrupt; the social contract is violated, social and political tension is increased. Society no longer feels protected by its institutions, representative democracy reveals its perverse core and the emperor is left without clothes.

Utopia as negation of the current order (Löwy, 2008) and as a door half-open (Bloch I: 387) is present in the work of liberation theologists, in the search for possibilities of the not-yet-concrete. There are certainly eschatological and epistemological differences among them, but they are similar in their thinking of the interests of the victims. It is precisely this relation with the victims that not only makes it an attractive proposal but also valid and necessary in the struggles for liberation.

Utopia and the politics of liberation are found actively participating in Boff's theological and ethical tenets with the intention of confronting the hegemonic discourse that promotes social conformity and abnegation. Boff refuses to accept that the suffering of millions of enslaved people, the Indigenous, the humiliated and offended of our history, has been in vain. For Boff (2006: 54), such suffering has accumulated force and many demands for transformation.

On 19 November 2004, Leonardo Boff published an article entitled 'De onde tirar esperança?' ('Where do we find hope?', Boff, 2004b), in which he expressed his surprise at the electoral ratification whereby the people of the United States reinstated George Bush and, most of all, his foreign policy that has provoked irreparable damage in the territories of peripheral nations. It is in this context that Boff asks: from where do we find hope? The response, inspired by Bloch, differentiated between the hope of those above and the hope of those from below.

> Are we going to find hope in religions and in Churches, because, as Ernst Bloch said with reason, 'Where there is religion, there is hope'? In fact, for the truly poor, the Churches become their refuge, the place where they find some hope, even though it may be filled with out of the world beliefs, alienated from the historical processes and compromises with social change. But even in that hope they find some reason for life. Regrettably, to many of these Churches the Spanish saying applies: 'Between God and money, the second is first.' The source of hope resides in the victims themselves. Hope is the only thing the victims have: hope that, no matter how adverse reality is, something good will come of it. That hope against all hope carries the fundamental utopia that one day everybody will have something to eat, everybody will have a home, everybody will be able to see the doctor and enjoy good health, all the children will go to school … The hope that we will drink a beer with our friends on Friday afternoons and, perhaps, a retirement check may bring tranquillity to our old age. And finally, this is what the poor think: that humanity can be a family, living all together on planet Earth as brothers and sisters. (Neither Bush nor Blair, and least of all our power and social elites think like that.) Are not the poor those who remind us that, 'Hope is the last thing to die'? (Boff, 2014)

Concrete utopia and faith as a utopic function for the emancipation of the victims of capital – that is, the poor and the Earth, have been assimilated by the liberationist *locus* with planetary and ecological tints given by Leonardo Boff. The ex-Franciscan insists on the construction of a bio-civilisation which would incorporate a new relation with nature. The rainbow, as an image (*Weltbild*) of plurality serves as a metaphor for the concordance among diverse movements (pacifist, ecological, LGBT, socialist, among others), and is a horizon which we should follow, as we need a change of civilisation. In this sense, the rainbow should be understood more as a dialectical image rather than a point of destiny.

Philosophy and Trans-modernity

Towards the end of the 1970s, Enrique Dussel participated in a debate with Marcel Xhafflaire on the potential of infrastructural religion[50] in the processes of liberation. Using contributions from Feuerbach, Luxemburg, Lenin, Gramsci and Ernst Bloch,[51] Dussel rebukes Xhafflaire for not considering that prophecy is constantly being renewed in the imaginary of the oppressed in order to rejuvenate their utopias and dreams of liberation.

In the same work, Dussel (1977: 82–83) alludes to the relation between nature and humankind. While conducting an in-depth hermeneutic on the sacrament of baptism, Dussel states that:

> Not only does water have physical effects upon people but moral and intellectual effects as well. Water not only cleanses the body of impurities; water cleanses the eyes, allowing us to see clearly, to feel more free; water extinguishes the heat of lust ... Water is the first aid closest to nature ... Morality is nothing without nature, it must be linked with the simplest forms of nature ... Our symbols are wine and bread. These are, on account of matter, products of nature and on account of form products of men. If we, in reference to water, have said that man cannot live without nature – in terms of spirituality, for bread and wine we say: nature is nothing without humankind; nature needs humans, as humans need nature.[52]

Enrique Dussel (1985) maintains that *The philosophy of liberation* was a spin-off in the 1970s of the treatment of two problems: on the one hand, the situation of poverty affecting a large part of humanity and, on the other, environmental degradation, both of which are caused by capitalist production. For Dussel (1985: 140), the political liberation of the periphery is a necessary condition for any ethical or ontological project that pushes for the construction of a real democratic (not in the bourgeois sense) society. Here, Dussel identifies the need for a trans-modern project on behalf of the victims.[53]

Hegemonic modernity, as a Eurocentric project, came out of the negation of ontological statutes, as well as the material possibilities for reproduction of Black people, Indigenous peoples, women and nations of the periphery. Said project implied the bases of expansion of the economic system (mercantile capitalism) and a pattern of domination (Lusitanian-Hispanic colonialism) that would continue to impose costs on the victims in the aftermath of the twentieth century. Thus, in contrast to the postmodern current that has disdain for emancipatory projects – throwing away the baby with the bathwater – the philosophy of liberation claims the liberationist side of *ratio* and drives towards a symmetric dialogue among victims who, for the last five centuries, have been excluded from the whole of hegemony. This reasoning and dialogue are made possible in a trans-modern project (Dussel, 2003).

The Word: Between God and Liberation

The violence exercised by the power of imposition on the part of the political-military class and North American consultancy under the National Security Doctrine (Rockefeller Report, 1969; see Cockcroft, 2001), has been documented by various political, social and intellectual actors in order to denounce impunity.[54] Memory, as an element of resistance, is fundamental to the strategies of social emancipation. Since it is a social product, memory also contains contradictions (abstract utopias, dreams, fetishised images) that mobilise or encapsulate the historical dynamic.

The role that the Church played in legitimising or confronting the logic of domination has been tackled from different perspectives.[55] The political commitment, adopted, and even brought to the level of sacrifice, by some prophetic figures of Latin American Catholicism, represented one of the most beautiful pages of Church history in that region. So, based on Bloch's contributions, we undertake deep hermeneutics in order to trace the presence of the utopic function in the literature of liberation theology. The Principle of Hope, as a 'main drive for a dream ahead' (Bloch, 1996) can be revealed in the poetry of Ernesto Cardenal and Frei Tito, and in the narratives provided by Frei Betto.

For Bloch, the artisitic appearance as a visible pre-appearance is another configuration of the utopic dynamic. In this sense, resting on Scaliger,[56] Bloch maintains that the poet holds the *creator spiritus*, that creative spirit as a utopic totem which behaves as a subversive demonic element. The poet, thus, is not only the carrier of the spirit of his/her times but also the causing actor in the prefiguration of concrete utopias. That is, a seer of a classless society.

Liberating-prophetic poetry has found one of its great expressions in the work of Ernesto Cardenal.[57] This Nicaraguan priest incorporated himself into the Trappist order at Our Lady of Gethsemane in Kentucky, where Thomas Merton[58] served as his counsellor. Years later, following a period of illness, he established himself at the Benedictine monastery of Santa María de la Resurrection in Cuernavaca. It is worth mentioning here that some of the Beat Poets spent time at this monastery. Thereafter, Cardenal studied theology at the Cristo Sarcedote Seminary in Antioquia, Colombia – one of the most progressive institutions of the time – and this is where he became a priest in 1965. Thereafter, he returned to Nicaragua with the intention of establishing a contemplative and self-sufficient community on the island of Solentiname. This would become the meeting place of such intellectuals as Julio Cortázar and José Coronel Ultrecho, among others. During those years he was drawn to Marxism and became involved in the Sandinista Front. Some of the members of the community became leaders in that political organisation.

The Arrival
We get off the plane and we go, Nicaraguans and foreigners,
all mixed together toward the huge lighted building – first stop
Immigration and Customs – and as we approach, passport in hand,
I think of how proud I am to be holding
the passport of my socialist country, and of my satisfaction
at arriving in a Socialist Nicaragua. 'Brother'
they'll say to me – a revolutionary brother welcomed
by the revolutionary brothers of Immigration and Customs –
not that there won't be controls; there must be controls
so that capitalism and Somozaism never come back –
and the emotion of coming back to my country during a revolution
with more changes, more and more decrees
of expropriation that I'd hear of, changes more and more radical,
many surprises in the short time I've been away
and I see joy in the eyes of everybody – the ones that have stayed,
the others are gone already – and now we go into the brightness
and they ask natives and foreigners for their passports ...
but it was all a dream and I am in Somoza's Nicaragua
and they take away my passport with the icy courtesy

with which Security would tell me 'Please come in'
and they take the passport inside and they don't bring it back (surely
they must surely be phoning Security
or the Presidential Palace or somebody or other) and by now
all the other passengers are gone and I don't know if I'll be arrested
but no: at the end of an hour they come back with my passport.
The CIA must have known that this time I didn't go to Cuba
and that I was just a single day in East Berlin,
and so at last I can go through Customs
all alone in Customs with my ancient suitcase
and the kid that inspects just pretends to inspect
without inspecting anything and he murmurs to me: 'Father'
and he doesn't dig deep down into the suitcase where he would find
the phonograph record with Allende's last appeal to the people
from the Palace, interrupted by the sound of bombs exploding,
the record I bought in East Berlin, or Fidel's speech
about Allende's overthrow, the one Sergio gave me,
and the kid says: 'It's eight o'clock already and we haven't had supper,
us customs workers get hungry, too.'
'What time do you have your supper?' I ask 'Not till after the last plane
    lands'
and now I'm moving toward the dark demolished city
where everything is just the same and nothing's going on but I have seen
his eyes and with his eyes he has said to me: 'Comrade.'
(Cardenal, 1977: 68)

We randomly select four sentences from this poem to reveal some utopic elements which take part of the Nicaraguan imaginary. The first: 'but it was all a dream and I am in Somoza's Nicaragua'. Dreaming is a compensatory mechanism by which the subconscious works out features repressed by the conscious. Desires, fear, projections of what Lacan would call the *petit objet*, elaborated through onerous language, strategies of escape or of irruption. Nevertheless, the neurosis or crisis (psychiatric or social) produces moments of transition. Transition is always a path towards change. One's reaction to crisis always depends on the subject (ego), on its circumstances (superego) and its it (id). In this line, we see the form in which the subject recognises his place of enunciation: Somoza's Nicaragua, Nicaragua of reproach, of shame and of terror.

The second: 'we get hungry'. For Bloch (I, 1996: 94), the question of hunger has been circumvented by hegemonic ontology. Its absence is due to the neo-Platonic heritage of separating soul-body and spirit. However, in material terms, hunger has been a constant for the countries of the periphery. It is no coincidence that Nicaragua, during the time of Somoza, was one of those countries with the worst gap between rich and poor. Third: 'What time do you have your supper?' This is a call to action, to praxis. The difference between natural history (passive subject) and history as social production lies in the concrete intervention *ad hominem*. Finally, 'and with his eyes he has said to me: "Comrade".' According to Emmanuel Levinas (1991), the look is an opening; it is transcendental with regard to the other. Nonetheless, the word 'comrade' provides a subversive gradient to Levinas' de-politicised relational ontology.

In the community of Solentiname, Cardenal set up programmes of poetry and painting for the people of Nicaragua. At the start of the revolution, Anastasio Somoza Debayle (Tachito), son of the former dictator, bombed the community. For this reason, Cardenal went to Costa Rica in exile before going back to be named Minister of Culture by the revolutionary government. In his *Epigramas* (in Cardenal, 1999), he repudiates the dictatorship of Anastasio Somoza and expresses his sympathy for the resistance. His choice of words is significant, though: howl, wailing, tyrant, death: dictator. All of these undoubtedly infer not only an ontological suffering but a situation of generalised anguish.

> Suddenly in the night the sirens
> sound their long, long, long alarm,
> the siren's miserable *howl*
> of fire, or death's white ambulance
> like a ghost *wailing* in the night,
> coming closer and closer above the streets
> and the house, it rises, rises, and falls
> and it grows, grows, falls and goes away
> growing and dying. It's neither a fire nor a death:
> Just the Dictator flashing by.
> (Cardenal, 1977: 10)

Another one reads:

> We wake up with guns going off
> And the dawn alive with planes –

It sounds like a revolution:
It's only the Tyrant's birthday.
(Cardenal, 2009: 45–46)

In his collection of poetry, *Zero hour*, Cardenal (1980) writes a critique of Central America's condition, US intervention, the floating sovereignty of a dependent country, and he expresses his admiration for the figure of Augusto César Sandino.

He is a *bandido*', said Somoza, 'a *bandolero*.'
And Sandino at no time owned any property.
Which, translated into Spanish, means,
Somoza called Sandino a *bandolero*.
And Sandino never held any property,
And Moncada called him a bandit at banquets,
and Sandino in the mountains went without salt
and his men were shaking with cold in the mountains
and he mortgaged the house of his father-in-law
in order to free Nicaragua, while in the Presidential Palace
Moncada had mortgaged all of Nicaragua.
'Of course he isn't really', the American Minister declared
with a laugh, 'but we call him an outlaw in the technical
sense.'[59]

His *Salmos* (Psalms) (in Cardenal, 1999) are a combination of liberation theology, Latin American Marxism and Catholicism dedicated to social change. For example, 'Salmo 57' shows the relation between bourgeois law and the logic of capitalist exploitation, religion as the opium of the ruling classes counterposed to religion as the liberator of the oppressed and the realisation of the 'Kingdom of God'.

The masses shall have fun in exclusive clubs
They will take private enterprise into their possession
The just will be happy in the Popular Courts
We shall celebrate the Revolution's anniversary in big squares
The God who exists belongs to the proletariat.
(Cardenal, 1999; original translation)

With a revolutionary vision of the 'Good News', Cardenal wrote his *Gospel in Solentiname* (2006), which is a work influenced by Marxism and Latin American Catholic radicalism of the periphery.[60] Concrete utopia is understood in that text. The relation between this priest and the people is that of a prophet who confronts the status quo.

From Fortaleza, Brazil, Tito de Alencar Lima experienced the horrors of the military regime.[61] A member of the Catholic Students' organisation Juventud Estudiantil Católica, Frei Tito went to São Paulo in 1967, where he got involved in the student movement. A few years later, on the morning of 4 November, a certain Sérgio Paranhos Fleury broke into the Dominican convent in order to detain him – that was when the torture began. At Tiradentes prison, in São Paulo, Frei Tito stoically endured physical and psychological torture. Nevertheless, Frei Tito never renounced the dream of the 'Kingdom of God' concretised in the construction of a democratic, free (not in the abstract sense), egalitarian and socialist society *tout court*. The love for music, poetry, walks in the countryside and prayer were key to the life of the Dominican friar.

> **Se o Céu o a Terra**
> **(If Heaven and Earth)**
> Se minh'alma é morta, quem a ressucitá?
> (If my soul is dead, who will resuscitate it?)
> De noites sombrias
> (Of sombre nights)
> De luzes opacas.
> (of opaque lights.)
> Meu espírito geme em dores.
> (My spirit moans in pain)
> Meu coração bate como tic-tac de um relógio
> (My heart beats like the ticking of a clock)
> Em busca do ser quando este ser é o nada.
> (In search of being when being is nothing.)
> Minha vida encerra-se em um eterno dilema:
> (My life becomes an eternal dilemma)
> O ser e o não-ser,
> (Being is non-being)
> Viver é ver,
> (Living is seeing)
> Ver estrelas,

(To see stars,)
Ver flores,
(To see flowers,)
Ver a infinita beleza de um ser criador.
(To see the infinite beauty of a creator-being.)
Nao busco o céu, mas talvez a terra,
(I do not search for heaven but perhaps for Earth)
Um paraiso perdido.
(A paradise lost.)
Se o céu é terra, nele eu me movo como um ser
(If heaven is Earth, I move in it as a being)
Moribundo: experiência, experiência de meu viver.
(Dying: experience of my living.)
Em luzes e trevas derrama o sangue da minha existencia.
(The blood of my existence is spilled in light and darkness.)
Quem me dirá como é o existir
(Who will tell me how to exist?)
Experiência do visível ou do invisível?
(Experience of the visible or the invisible?)
Se o invisível é visível, para que ver?
(If the invisible is visible, why then should I see?)
Meu ver é sofrer, num mundo oculto
(My sight is suffering in a hidden world)
De minha profundeza: minha singularidade.
(Of my deepness: my solitude)
Tal vez minha simplicidade complicada.
(Perhaps my complicated simplicity.)
Há razões para não-ser,
(There are reasons for not being,)
Pois no nada, no vazio,
(In nothingness, in a vaccum,)
Encontre uma chama que apanhe um absoluto.
(I found a flame that holds absoluteness.)
Mas aonde?
(But where?)
Em que terra?
(In what land?)
Olho todos os dias as estrelas, olhar singelo
(Every day I look at the stars, a simple look)

De um infinito, tão vasto quanto a distância de seu brilho.
(At an infinite so vast as their shining)
Talvez eles sejam os olhos de Deus, do Deus criador.
(Perhaps they are the eyes of God, God the creator).[62]

Once again, we shall examine four lines of this poem in order to understand the utopic urge in Frei Tito's existential anguish. *My spirit moans in pain*. In Semitic philology, spirit comes from the word *rúaj*, which means wind but also breath. In this sense, only a living organism and its symbiotic relation to its environment can carry spirit. For this reason, when life is found endangered or threatened, one reacts radically in the form of cries, moans, sobs. Thereafter, *To see stars*. For Bloch, stars are a utopic element *par excellence*. They guide our way, they move us, always unreachable but, by the same token, at the horizon to which we move. We could even say that it plays a role along the lines of *la femme introuvable* (Bloch III: 136), of the images of hope of a fulfilled moment. Thereafter, *a paradise lost* – a millennial expression that confronts the present with conviction. Last but not least, *Every day I look at the stars*. The perpetual search for a concrete historical present; the incessant hunt for residual utopia.

Carlos Alberto Libânio Christo, better known as Frei Betto, was born in 1944 in Belo Horizonte, Brazil and studied at Cristo Rei Jesuit seminary in São Leopoldo. Frei Betto was groomed by the prophetic figure of Camilo Torres of Leuven University. Frei Betto participated in helping many militants cross the border in their resistance to the military regime. The risks and the commitment of this Dominican friar also brought him to write his *Batismo de sangue* (1984). An avid reader of San Juan de la Cruz (St John of the Cross), Santa Teresa de Ávila, Saint Augustine, as well as Pascal, Marx, Lenin and Mao, among many others, Frei Betto brought the message of the Gospel to its ultimate consequences, committing to activities that sought the social and economic transformation of his country.

In *Batismo de sangue*, Frei Betto narrates the Calvary suffered by Dominican friars of the time, under political-military repression in what was known as Operação Bata Branca (Operation White Robe, in reference to the colour of their habit), which led them to join cause with the Bahia leader Carlos Marighella. Throughout the story, we perceive the utopic function in the religious as well as the laymen and their ethical-political locus: solidarity with the oppressed.

By way of fine prose, Frei Betto's enviable pen reveals humanity's existential anguish, the tormented being, the sacrificial victim, and denounces the discursive gadgets of the oppressor's system. The text is divided into six chapters that cover: the role of rural and urban guerrillas in Brazil, the presence of the CIA in matters of counter-insurgency, the captivity and confinement of Dominican friars, the death of anonymous martyrs, the forms of resistance and the solidarity of subjects in suspense. The writing is valuable, not only aesthetically but historically as well.

In chapter V, especially in sections 7, 8 and 9, we feel the heartbeat of the Christianity of Liberation. We witness a dialogue between Monsenhor Marcelo Pinto and Jeová de Assisi,[63] the interrogation of Frei Betto and the subversion of the first Christians during the Roman Empire; the elective affinity between Marxism and Christianity as ethical discourses and practices;[64] but most of all, the conviction that to transform society to the benefit of those from below is an ethical imperative and human necessity.

In 2006, Helvécio Ratton directed the film *Batismo de sangue*, based on Frei Betto's book, to expose the relation between the Dominican friars and the resistance movement (Ação Libertadora Nacional, led by Marighella) against the dictatorship. Frei Tito's suffering (played by Caio Blat), is axial in the film. Nevertheless, we can observe some of the methods of torture exercised by the military police, the Department of Social and Political Order (for which Firmino Perez Rodrigues was primarily responsible) and of the Navy. Throughout the film we witness the way in which students, workers, clergymen and women were tortured.[65] In one key scene, a certain official Fleury – Head of the Death Squads (Frei Betto, 1984: 93–97), played by Cássio Gabus Mendés, scolds Frei Tito and says: 'Traitor to the Church, traitor of Brazil.'[66] It would be certainly interesting to conduct an interpretive analysis of the differences and similarities that we find in the narrative's structure (film and book), but that would divert us from the central objective of this work: to understand the utopic function within resistance, in this case touched upon in the literary production of liberation theologists.

To conclude, we believe that the pertinence and relevance of *The principle of hope* is more than evident. Although the postmodern current proclaims the illegitimacy of the narrative of emancipation and one-track thinking trumpets the end of utopias, we remain convinced that the awakened dreams do not die in the face of hegemonic discourses, given that the utopic function is present in all human beings. For this reason, Ernst Bloch always highlighted the open character of utopias. For him, the utopic function is an anthropological and metaphysical principle among human beings, it is imperishable because a latent process exists in all beings-in-possibility towards the not-yet-achieved.[67] For this reason, we believe that Bloch's contribution lies in an exhortation towards action and the search for a true homeland (*patria*);[68] both path and journey are important factors in the dynamic of awakened dreams.

The awakened dreams of Latin American social movements of liberationist stock demonstrate that neither hope nor utopia succumb to the entelechies of dominant discourses. They are concrete utopias that take two of Bloch's concerns into consideration: hunger and dominated nature.[69]

From the perspective of critical Marxism, the works of Ernst Bloch continue to be of value, as they surpass the analytical reductionism that treats the religious phenomenon as a simple process of alienation. If Bloch recognised the alienating character of religion as an abstract utopia, he also looked at the critical-utopic aspect of religion as subversion. Alluding to the War of the Maccabees, the German peasant uprisings, the Anabaptist revolts, the Cathars and their ilk, Ernst Bloch shows how, at certain historical moments, religion (the messianic, prophecy, etc.) has nurtured diverse projects of popular demands. It is therefore no coincidence that the theologists and philosophers of liberation in Latin America found an important source of theory and eschatology in *The principle of hope*.

4

The Gun Powder of the Dwarf: Unearthly Reflections on Contemporary Political Philosophy

The story is told of an automaton constructed in such a way that it could play a winning game of chess, answering each move of an opponent with a countermove. A puppet in Turkish attire and with a hookah in its mouth sat before a chessboard placed on a large table. A system of mirrors created the illusion that this table was transparent from all sides. Actually, a little hunchback who was an expert chess player sat inside and guided the puppet's hand by means of strings. One can imagine a philosophical counterpart to this device. The puppet called 'historical materialism' is to win all the time. It can easily be a match for anyone if it enlists the services of theology, which today, as we know, is wizened and has to keep out of sight.

(Walter Benjamin, 1969: 253)

The twenty-first century heralded serious environmental damage, a significant increase in poverty and the highest levels of social exclusion that radically put into question the very paradigm of civilisation. In the light of current events that have arisen over recent years ('preventative' wars, treacherous massacres against civilian populations and the institutionalisation of the 'State of Exception' among others), it is important to ask ourselves about the role and contribution of philosophy and theology in the development of alternative projects and in counterposing the hegemonic narrative. Our purpose is to analyse, from political philosophy, the principal tenets of Slavoj Žižek, Enrique Dussel and Leonardo Boff, given that in their works they have never stopped reflecting on the injustices caused by the existing system, and proposing other forms of understanding what is political. Likewise, they demonstrate points of agreement and disagreement not just in theory but in strategy as well. Precisely for this reason, we will divide our *excursus* into three moments: in the first we will observe the theological exegesis that these authors use to construct the architecture of their discourse; and soon we will see the way of understanding the political, and its factual forms; and finally we will ponder the relevance of their proposals in the process of social transformation.

Undoubtedly, the choice to address these authors' theoretical proposals is a demonstration of our political and philosophical affiliations; moreover, this is about those thinkers considered to be representative in the current philosophical debate. Among the traits or common backgrounds we can see that they are people who originate from countries from the periphery and, because of that, their epistemic point is found in the borderlands of hegemonic thought. Therefore, as Bhabha (1995) maintains, the locus (or place) of enunciation is meaningful because it creates the conditions – whether material, subjective or discursive – of the enunciator.

While Enrique Dussel and Leonardo Boff were born in the Latin American periphery in the second half of the 1930s, Slavoj Žižek was born in the Euro-Asian periphery of the world-system at the end of the 1940s. While their basic education was developed in their respective countries, their 'stay in Western Europe' would significantly impact their intellectual production.

Although Slavoj Žižek graduated from the University of Ljubljana, his time in Paris was marked by the influence of Jacques Lacan. In fact, by 1966, in his famous work on *La Logique du fantasme,* Lacan confirms that he had created his greatest contribution in analytic theory, *l'objet a* (Assoun, 2009), a tool which is axial in the musings on the logic of culture, power and ideology in Žižek. Needless to say, the distinction between *l'imaginaire, du symbolique et du réel* is also subsumed in the perspective of this Slovenian thinker.

Enrique Dussel, on the other hand, lived for almost a decade in between Spain, France and Germany, and spent some time in Israel, where he discovered Emmanuel Levinas, who has been fundamental in his reading of Marxism. This stay was the result of writing his second work published in 1969 under the title *Semitic humanism*, where he underscores that the Semites conceive of man as indivisible, a posture *sui generis* between the anthropic dualism of the Greeks and the dualism or ontic-ethical hierarchical pluralism of Iranian religions (Dussel, 1969: 21).

Leonardo Boff completed his studies in Systemic Theology at Munich and earned his doctorate in 1970. Moreover, after concluding his doctoral studies, Ratzinger awarded him 14,000 Marks for the publication of his thesis because he considered it a great contribution to the field of ecclesiology (Tamayo, 1999: 150). We point out these episodes of intellectual biography because they demonstrate how these authors had Europe as a referential horizon. In another order of ideas, it is not a great stretch to refer to the research of Michael Löwy (1998) and Gerd-Rainer Horn (2008), which demonstrates the way in which French thinking influenced liberation theology in Latin America.

Critical Theologies

In *The puppet and the dwarf* (2003), Žižek reuses the image of the dwarf (*Zwerg*) of Walter Benjamin's first thesis on the philosophy of history to refer to the potential of theology in projects of political transformation. Žižek conducts a hermeneutic to demonstrate the indispensable union between Christianity and Marxism in the struggle against capitalism. It should be mentioned that, although Žižek is not a theologian by education, his exegesis of the Gospel is interesting and provocative because it argues that the subversive nucleus of Christianity can only be accessed through a materialist perspective. To him, only a materialist approach permits access to the heart (*Kern*) of Christianity and vice versa, or in other words, to be truly adept in dialectical materialism one should go through the experience of Christianity (2003: 3). He adds that, on the one hand, religion can also carry out a therapeutic function and, on the other, play a critical role in the prevailing social system.

On the theological level, this Slovenian thinker concentrates on the Letters of Paul of Tarsus. Žižek finds two angles to emphasise: (a) Paul is indifferent to the historic Jesus, meaning that he does not go in depth into the message of the Nazarene and (b) Paul is interested in the death on the cross and the resurrection that in some way will open the doors to start the organisation of the 'new party known as Christian communism' (2003: 9). In this sense, he turns to an examination of homologies between the work of Paul of Tarsus and that of Lenin.

Žižek maintains that after the 'Happening' (the October Revolution in the case of Russia), the true task is in maintaining the freedom that has been won. This point is significant because it marks the point of rupture with the messianic perspective of Judaism that awaits the arrival of the Messiah to forge redemption. Because of this, the Christian or Revolutionary Leninism era implies the defence, against all odds, of the 'Happening'. Although Žižek (2003) bases himself on the contributions of messianic Judaism (Benjamin or Rosenzweig) he distances himself from it when it comes to the 'Happening' (*l'Événement*) because, for him, the wait for the Messiah can be fixed into a passive position. However, this position can be debated because Michael Löwy (2009: 253) has demonstrated that the historic temporality (*historischer Zeitraffer*) of Benjamin's vision as an open process does not necessarily indicate a passivity on the part of human beings. Indeed, by the way, for Martin Buber, redemption can only be agreed upon with the participation of men (*mitwirkende Kraft*); this means an acting messianic force (Löwy, 2009: 63).

On the other hand, Žižek (2003) thinks that the book of Job is central in the critique of ideology because it demonstrates discursive strategies that legitimise suffering. In the dialogues with his friends – Eliphaz, Bildad and Zophar – Job argues about the absurdity of his suffering (Job 29:3–17, 31:16–24) and, far from being a passive victim, he challenges the Lord to demonstrate the incoherence of his suffering. Job does not accept the troubles in a spirit of abnegation; to the contrary, he wants to 'know' the cause of his malaise. He does not acquiesce in the discursive games of ideologues (Job 21:34) that want to justify his sorrows. In other words, Job is conscious that his situation is not logical.

The theology that Žižek proposes as an end is the *Che-isation* of Christ, that being a committed and subversive version of the Nazarene. For Žižek, the essential difference between the legitimate violence exercised by the 'Zen Guerrilla' and by the 'traditional West' is expressed in the 'act of love' (2003: 30–31). Violence in the revolutionary process implies a form of subjectivity-objectivity in which the individual produces itself. Žižek (2003: 175) confirms that for Fredric James, violence plays a role analogous to that of wealth in the Protestant legitimatisation of capitalism, since this does not have an intrinsic value and, therefore, should not be fetishised or celebrated per se; instead it is an authentic sign of the attempt for emancipation. In this same order of ideas, Žižek is convinced that the New Age phenomenon is the ideological expression of late capitalism, as it makes us participants in the neurotic dynamic of the system which both distances itself from, while being indifferent to structural violence.

Unlike Žižek, Enrique Dussel completed his studies in Science of Religion at the Catholic Institute of Paris and maintains that theology is the theoretical thinking that emerges from praxis and rests on the existential comprehension of the supernatural, that is, faith. Therefore, theology can be understood as an epistemic conceptualisation of the factual experience of Christian life. For Dussel (1992: 47) the famous 'theology of hope' of Jurgen Moltmann manifested the limits of Critical Theory of the Frankfurt School.

However, neither philosophical proposal surpassed ontology and the dialectic in what is considered in the future as Otherness (*Alteridad*). Both express the difficulty of proposing a political, economic, cultural and sexual *historical project of liberation* that would surpass that of the current Totality, being more concrete than that of the eschatological project. Because of this, Dussel insists that hope can attain an 'historical modification of life' but not a radical innovation of the current system, and that, without that concrete mediation, hope reaffirms the status quo and works as an opiate.

Dussel infers that if in the history of Christianity two Churches have existed, an imperial European one and another that is colonial-peripheral-Latin American, we can also detect the presence of two theologies. Rather than presenting a Manichaean view of reality, Dussel's intention is to demonstrate that theology is not neutral because, while being conditioned for the social-cultural space, its considerations will have limitations and, as a consequence, they will be specific. Because of this the theologian, philosopher or intellectual of the periphery has to respond to the questions not just of their time but also of their people.

A theology of the Third World has to have in mind this historical situation. It has to ask: 'What role has the Church been playing in this process in every phase and situation? How do Christians react to the phenomenon of the Western invasion of other lands? What was the prevalent theology? How is Christian theology related to the continued daily exploitation of the world? What does it give towards the construction of a just society? What contribution does the Church give to the liberation of oppressed people that have long suffered due to sexist, racist and classist domination? (Dussel, 1977: 256; original translation)

The use of passages of the Gospel has been very common in the philosophic and ethical propositions of this Argentinian thinker. However, a change in paradigm can be noted in the biblical references. While in the 1970s Dussel, under the influence of Rosenzweig, accentuated Easter (*pesah*) to refer to the process of the passage or path towards liberation, forged by the movements of decolonisation (in Algiers, Nicaragua, Vietnam, Cambodia, etc.) and critique of Totality, in Levinas's sense of the word, by way of a message of the Hebrew prophets (1 Sam. 8:18, Isa. 10:1), he currently reclaims the Gospel of Mark as the foundation of his politics of liberation. Following the Apostle Mark (10:42–44), Dussel (2007a: 39) differentiates between 'fetishised' power and 'obedient' power in the political expressions of the rulers. 'Political authority' is conceived as the ability of representatives to carry out the people's demands. In that respect, Juan Jose Tamayo (1999: 23) points out that theologian Carlos Bravo has presented the same gospel as a history of the liberating practices of Jesus that were violently truncated.

Dussel has linked the logic of capitalism and the dynamic of colonialism with the epiphany of modernity. To him, modernity is an historic and cultural process that finds its beginning in the 'discovery' of America, the 'hiding of the other' and its starting point is the Conquest. The *ego conquiro* of Hispanic-Lusitanian power created a society where the non-White person would be objectified as an object of production. Nevertheless, in this process of colonisation there was no absence of clergy who harshly criticised the methods of submission and domination. We are thinking of Bartolomé de las Casas in Chiapas, Juan del Valle in Popayan or Antonio de Valdivieso in Nicaragua (Dussel, 1992: 96). It is precisely from the first of these bishops that Dussel (2007a: 25) uses the concept of *consensus populi* to designate the consensual legitimacy or pact between the governors and the governed.

For his part, Brazilian theologian Leonardo Boff has deepened the reflection and scholastic practice. His first works, such as *Jesus Christ liberator* or *Gospel of the cosmic Christ*, established his principal proposals. Tamayo (1999: 56) writes about this, saying that Boff has been one of the principal parties responsible for the change of paradigm in modern Christology. 'We should', writes Boff (2004a: 236) 'overcome the anthropocentrism of the Christologies, because when Christ was deified he did not only liberate human beings but all the beings of the universe.'

Genesis is one of the books most covered by Leonardo Boff (1993: 46) in his ethical-ecological proposal. There we find a certain basis for understanding to what extent Judeo-Christianity is responsible for the ecological crisis. Boff underscores that on the one hand (Gen. 1:26–28) there comes about the power that man has over nature (*subjugai a terra e domina*); on the other hand, he also holds that man should cultivate and care for the Garden of Eden (Gen. 2:15). It is for this reason that Boff declares that a holistic interpretation can contribute to overcoming a reductionist and instrumental reading of said book.

For Boff (2004a), religion has been distorted theologically by power, to legitimise injustices, treacheries and abominations of the system. The Brazilian theologian marks out six anti-ecological points of the Judeo-Christian tradition: patriarchy, monotheism, anthropocentrism, ethnocentrism (notion of the chosen people), the disdain for the material (Gen. 6:13) and the concept of the 'fallen nature' or, in other words, that the universe was corrupted by the devil due to original sin.

The sixteenth century inaugurated the expansion of the project of power-domination by Western culture. Just like Dussel, Leonardo Boff (2000: 98) admits that the maxim *'ego conquiro'* tainted in great measure the philosophic basis of modernity in the expressions of its proponents, René Descartes and Francis Bacon. In other words, modernity contributes to the disdain for nature that reduces it to an object for pillage.

Politic(s)

Žižek (2007) places the birth of 'politics' in the Hellenic world from a Hegelian approach, and conceives of it as a process where an explosive short circuit is created between the individual and the universal, or when the useless parts of the social body are repositioned inside of the socio-political apparatus. Still today, the political sphere has been absorbed by the economic and, therefore, a politicisation of the economy is necessary. That is possible only by decoding the system's discursive paradigm. In this sense, Žižek manifests his distrust for the policies that come from multiculturalism, and includes the civil alternatives like the World Social Forum with those that he has designated under the label of 'the good men of Porto Davos' (Žižek, 2006).

The 'Happening' of history was the October Revolution. The party's task implied the defence and internationalisation of the communist project. Like St Paul, Vladimir Ilyich Ulyanov attempted to convert unbelievers. For this reason, Žižek affirms that the betrayal of Judas is similar to that of Stalin. A real 'Che-isation' of Christ consists in unveiling the perverse nucleus of the postmodern ideology and its sinister dynamics of *anything goes*. The Paulist-Leninist message implies maintaining a politically justified intolerance towards the measures put forth by *affirmative action* or *positive discrimination,* as they only contribute to the reification of the system. Class struggle is not only valid, it is necessary. For Žižek (2001: 2) we should cling to the challenges of religious heritage at the bosom of Marxism because Christianity and Marxism can fight together; behind the barricades we see the coming of 'new spiritualities' and fundamentalist *freaks*. The authentic Christian legacy is too valuable to be abandoned to the perverse multicultural discourses. According to Žižek (2001: 10) the term 'worker' has disappeared significantly from the current critical and political discourse to the benefit of the word 'immigrant', and in this way the problems of class – which inherently imply exploitation – are transformed into multicultural problems, which results in the reconfiguring of the liberal discourses

The Paulist vision of history, according to Žižek (2009: 44) helps us to unravel the false problem of humanisation, given that when Saint Paul says that 'There are no Greeks, nor Jews, nor women nor men,' it does not mean that we should all be 'one' happy family. Instead it means that unity is threatened by individual identities and so 'There are no Greeks, nor Jews, nor men or women, there are only Christians and enemies of Christianity' should be interpreted as them being on one side, those that fight for emancipation and, on the other side, their reactionary opponents. In political terms, there are the people and the enemies of the people.

In another order of ideas, for Žižek, the only way of combating the hegemonic system is to resort to the teachings of Lenin. The creation of a strong party, disciplined and with all the courage to destroy the enemy is the task to be completed. Hence orthodoxy (here he depends on Chesterton) and the respect of law are fundamental[1] in the transformative process of the 'class of itself' into 'class for itself', ergo, the concept of class and its manifestation in the process of struggle should be renewed in the political proposals that strive for radical transformation of society. For Žižek (2003) true ethical action does not consist in saving the most number of victims but in the decided will – even without scruples – of eliminating those guilty of transforming them into victims.

Enrique Dussel has dedicated his work to undoing Eurocentrism and Hellenic-centrism in philosophy. All of the political philosophies en vogue have always started in Greece. However, when you speak of *demo*-cracy, you forget that the Greek work *demos* is of Egyptian origin, in the old Egyptian language *dmi* meaning village. The word *dike* (divine justice) also did not have Hellenistic roots because it came from the Acadian *duku*, which means it is Semitic. 'In this way', says Dussel:

> we can destroy, de-construct, one-by-one the most technical words, those most fundamental to Greek politics, which have their origin in the Egyptian, Mesopotamian, Phoenician, Semitic world, and from the Bronze Age and the third and second millennium before Christ, in the territory that was later occupied by barbarian invaders like the Greeks. (Dussel, 2007b: 11)

We note this because it seems to us that there is a substantial difference from Žižek's perspective.

Dussel (2007b) maintains that modern politics are founded in the pragmatic domination that the Hispanic and Lusitanian conquistadors employed in the sixteenth century. The *ego conquiro* (1521–34) would, after a century, become the Cartesian *ego cogito* (1636), determinant in the classic definitions of modern political philosophy. One of these definitions is that which conceives of 'power' as a synonym of domination. However, Dussel suggests that social movements need a different theoretical framework, made of other categories and other concepts, so that they are able to articulate their demands with an anti-hegemonic political horizon.

The political community, Dussel (2006: 26) argues, is the only source of power; so, in other words, the legitimacy of power is found in the people. Dussel distinguishes between *potencia* and *potestas* to explain the performative logic in the political field. According to this author, the community or the people (*pueblo*) need politics to assure their own reproduction as a group. 'The will to live' helps them look for mechanisms and forms of organisation that can regulate the 'common good', the best way possible. The *potentia* is the contents, not yet concretised, of their capacity for transformation or social management. However, to produce a solution to their demands the community needs to delegate tasks, be it through consensually created institutions or through certain individuals. *Potestas* is the 'delegated power' by the political community to those governing. Dussel (2006: 36) points out that the 'government' comes from the Greek word *gobernao* which means 'to pilot a boat'. In this sense, the community is in charge of choosing and designating the rulers who will make public decisions.

The Gospel of Mark (10: 41) is very clear in pointing out that the authorities should serve others. The government is ultimately the servant of the public and should report to the political community that has elected it; and, at the moment where it 'fetishises power' and exercises pure domination, a flow is broken between the political community (*potentia*) and the government (*potestas*), at which point, the people become actors in rebellion and depose their mandatories. The 'state of rebellion' and liberating power of the people is diametrically opposed to the 'state of exception' of corrupted power, given that it is the moment in which the victims face their assassins and make them abdicate, it is the critical consensus of the denied (Dussel, 2006: 96) that unite to propagate a new hegemony. Here, Dussel reclaims Gramsci's concept of the 'historical bloc of the oppressed' to subsume that of 'class'.

Contextualising geopolitically the struggles for liberation in the periphery, Dussel does not dismiss the concept of class. To the contrary, he is convinced that the 'historical bloc' articulates the notion of class and that of the people. He differs from Žižek in aspects of organisation and political tactics, because for Dussel social movements (MST, the Neo-Zapatistas, Cocaleros Movement, among others) are the historical subjects that today are transforming the classic form of understanding politics and its pragmatics.

For his part, Leonardo Boff (2006: 58) explains that:

When we speak about the people, we do so not in the sense of rhetoric, but in the sense of social analysis: the people as that part of the population that were previously a mass, and that, in light of new consciousness and in organising a network of movements and united communities for a common dream ... [t]his part of the population that takes up the cause of the other part, those that have not yet been able to organise themselves, and then represents them. All of them, the organised and the unorganised but represented, are now political actors. The new State assumes the people's project and then creates the conditions for implementation. The State is, then, no longer the great obstacle to necessary changes, but an ally and instrument for making them reality. Because of this, the people, as the actor, should be heard. (original translation)

Coming from a liberationist perspective, Boff (1993: 133) proposes the establishment of the new social contract that should surpass the anthropocentrism – belonging to a reductionist vision of religion – that has so damaged thee *dignitas Terrae*. This does not omit the defence of human rights, the promotion of participatory democracy or the respect for cultural diversities. On the contrary, it inscribes them into a wider political project in an environment of universal validity, where the criteria of truth is life, real concrete life.

> Each specific oppression also calls for a specific liberation. However we cannot lose sight of the fact that the fundamental oppression is socio-economic. The others are all over-determinants of this base oppression. The socio-economic oppression goes back to class struggle and, in it, the groups express their antagonism and their irreconcilable interests. The exploited worker in our system can never reconcile with the exploiting employer. This socio-economic oppression heightens the other oppressions, as Black people, Indigenous peoples and women are dominated more when they are exploited and impoverished. (Boff, 1993: 133; original translation)

Boff (2004a: 152) makes clear that, since its epiphany, liberation theology has broken with the Church's paternalistic posture, as it did not condemn the 'structural sin'; that is, the capitalist system which causes social injustices, economic inequalities and juridical asymmetries. However, through the Ecclesiastical Grassroots Communities, as Brazilian theologies espouse, liberation theology participates in the production of the most democratic and participatory forms of community life, resulting in a joint effort with other social struggles. There are countless numbers of moments or processes in which the Ecclesiastical Grassroots Communities have played a decisive role in Latin America (Löwy, 1998).

It might prove interesting to observe that Boff (2000: 47) also rescues the charismatic figures of Lenin, Che Guevara and Chico Mendes in order to outline his prophetical political project of liberation, in which the goal is to unite marginalised groups through a process of conscious-raising and the creation of organic organisations that are bent on the radical transformation of society, in which the importance of leadership is fundamental in the emancipation process.

In a counter-position to Žižek, Boff suggests that the World Social Forum is an important space where social movements, marginalised groups and civil society organisations that believe 'another world is possible' can have dialogue and learn from their different experiences of struggle. In this sense, it would seem that liberation theology not only remains discursively valid but continues to be articulated in the social movements of the periphery.

Horizons of Liberation

Žižek (2009: 154) reclaims the revolutionary project of communism. Leaning on Lacan, however, he holds that desire (*désir*) should not outline our concept of happiness (*bonheur*), as it is anchored in society and its contradictions, so it does not escape the process of alienation. Taking up the notion of *homo sacer*, Žižek (2003) suggests that, in the current context, it is expressed by the figure of the 'happy moron'; that is, the individual that supposes s/he can be fulfilled individually and psychologically through consumption.

The 'really existing Christianity' (Žižek, 2003: 53) has not only neutralised its subversive and protesting nucleus, but moreover, it has supported the projects of the dominant classes. In this sense, he concludes that, more than maintaining a paternalistic position, the true task does not consist in obtaining compensation from the responsible parties, but in keeping them from their position which enables them to be responsible. Therefore, instead of asking for compensation from God, or from the elites, we should ask ourselves if we really need him or them. The destruction of private property and the old economic, political and ideological structures is an urgent task, and said task can only be carried out through the creation of a strong party, intolerant of the reforms that the dominant classes sometimes offer and the minimal demands of the multicultural proposal. Just like Lenin, Žižek maintains a distrust of the spontaneity of social movements that are considered flighty and easy to manipulate.

The trans-modernity that Dussel proposes implies the convergence of the groups that are found outside of totality (the Indigenous in the colonial framework, women in the patriarchal context, Black people in the racial field, the poor in the capitalist system, etc.) in a counter-hegemonic project that can include the victims of modernity. *Ratio* as an instrument of liberation should not be underestimated; instead, it should be exercised as a discursive strategy that causes the least harm or, in other words, it should exclude the least possible number. The philosophy of liberation that Dussel has cultivated since the 1970s was founded in a discursive ethics that openly confronts the proposals of the centre (for example those of Apel and Habermas), because he considers them to be charged with a metaphysical individualism that makes them fall into a reductionist formalism. Dussel begins with the 'suffering body' (*corporalidad sufriente*) of those excluded by the current system, and maintains that human rights cannot be postulated a priori, as does natural law. Instead, human rights are a result of a specific historic process and, in this sense, should be created a posteriori. Through critical political consciousness, on behalf of the groups 'without rights', and struggle – state of rebellion – for their recognition, it would be possible to see a 'state of law' that is more democratic.

In contrast to Žižek, Dussel affirms that if it is difficult to translate the demands of the different social movements into a hegemonic project, it is possible to make a common programme of diverse demands, and the World Social Forum is an example. However, the struggle of the social movements in different moments (elections, uprisings, revolutions, etc.) is still a *sine qua non* for social transformation.

Leonardo Boff suggests that the sixteenth century marked the initial expansion of Western domination, establishing asymmetric social relations between two worlds that are completely different from each other. The colonial wound is still present in the Latin American collective social imagination, and is expressed not only in the transference of value towards the countries of the core but in the daily racism that rules such societies. Given this, the Brazilian theologian strives for a 'founding break' (2006: 51) that would cement a new social contract. However, this not only should be between people but also between human beings and nature.

The split between the material and the spirit should be transcended by a holistic vision which relates the parts with the purpose of demonstrating the cosmic process that human life follows. In that direction, Boff (1993: 18, 2004a: 65) relies on the philosophic tenets of the South African philosopher Jan Smuts. Nonetheless, it is important to state clearly that the Brazilian theologian does not assimilate them apolitically, as do the followers of deep ecology; instead, he does so in order to articulate an emancipatory political project. It is worth mentioning that Boff is a member of the Eco-Socialist Network of Brazil.

Just like Dussel, Boff spares no expense in the defence and promotion of human rights. So much so that we should point out that, in 1979, he participated in the foundation of the Centre for the Defence of Human Rights in Petropolis. Hence, Boff serves as a palpable example of the ethical-political commitment of the intellectual to his people and his history; because, according to him, the intersection of theory and praxis is the only method for social transformation. Nevertheless, his commitment to the cause of the poor brought him on two occasions (1984 and 1992) to face accusations from the Holy Congregation for the Doctrine of Faith.

To conclude, we believe that these authors' proposals should be confronted at 'ground-level'; meaning that not only should they be examined with regard to their potential for emancipation but also their pertinence in the current social historic context. In this respect, we believe that Žižek's proposal is provocatively seductive but it is not completely useful for the processes through which the social struggles are passing in the periphery. Although we accept his reading on 'false illusions', which only lead to reform of the system, we infer that, in the end, history is struggle and movement. In this sense, there is nothing established and historical change will come out of the relation of forces. We consider, unlike liberation theology, that Liberation Philosophy is weak in not having identified itself with the social movements. Because of this, we can warn that the political-intellectual backgrounds of the authors we have analysed influence not only their proposals but also their strategies for struggle.

To readdress the excellent exegesis 'Sur le concept d'histoire de Walter Benjamin' carried out by Michael Löwy (2007b: 33), we are convinced that theology has to be at the service of the oppressed, as this dwarf can re-establish the explosive, messianic and revolutionary charge of historic materialism; that being to keep the gun powder safe from the torrential rains of mechanical materialism. Therefore, with the help of the dwarf and his gun powder, we can achieve human emancipation, meaning implement a true state of exception; that this would not, finally, be a divine one, but cooperation between God and human being.

5

Tendencies and Latencies of Liberation Theology in the Twenty-First Century

The French-Brazilian sociologist Michael Löwy distinguishes between *liberation theology* and *liberation Christianity* to explain the socio-historical movement of the late 1960s in Latin America. For Löwy (1998: 53), Liberation Christianity is a deeper phenomenon, which also includes Protestants and lay people, and allowed the emergence of liberation theology in the early 1970s. In this sense, Liberation Christianity (as a conceptual term) achieves an articulation of the elements that subsequently composed liberation theology, that is, it refers to a fixed worldview.

For Löwy, the emergence of the Catholic left in Brazil in the 1960s was the first manifestation of what would later become known as Liberation Christianity. That movement is a set of ideas and practices that challenge social injustice and, therefore, involves a commitment on the part of Christians, clergy members and laity organised in Ecclesiastic Grassroots Communities (EGCs), popular congregations, Catholic University Youth (CUY), Young Catholic Workers (YCW) and grassroots educational movements. It is evident that the issue of poverty has been a concern of the Catholic Church. However, from the liberationist perspective the poor are not considered as an 'object' of aid, but as an historical subject and, therefore, actors in their own liberation.

The particular historical constellation that allowed the emergence of Liberation Christianity was, first, the internal transformation of the Church (with the election of Pope John XXIII in 1958), which contributed to the creation of the Vatican Council II and, moreover, the triumph of the Cuban revolution of 1959 because, through its anti-imperialist agenda, it opened up the cycle of social struggles and popular uprisings (Löwy, 2007c: 306–18).

Critique of Capitalism as Religion

Liberation theology, as a critical and emancipatory discourse, has been instrumental in the process of hegemonic narrative *de-fetishisation*. Through a prophetic[1] and subversive look at the various aspects of modern society – the sanctification of the market, messianic technology, the myth of progress, the ideology of developmentalism, among others – this liberation theology has revealed the sacrificial character of the hegemonic system. Although we have no doubt that liberation theology is not an homogeneous current of thought, we sustain that its matrix or mythical-ontological-ethical[2] nucleus is mediated by a liberating critical locus. Hence, as Jung Mo Sung (2008: 34) masterfully explains, the impact of dependency theory on the analytical mediation of liberation theologists. For Sung, the dependency theorists are mainly divided into two groups, one which holds that development is not feasible under the capitalist system which raises the need for socialist revolution (Theotonio dos Santos, Rui Mauro Marini and André Gunder Frank), and those who disagree with that thesis (Celso Furtado, Fernando H. Cardoso, Aníbal Pinto, Osvaldo Sunkel and Enzo Falleto). Hence, the theoretical inclination towards certain analytical tools on the part of liberation theologists permeates their socio-religious exegesis.

Since the late 1980s, liberation theologists have underlined the idolatrous character of capitalism. For them, the central problem in Latin America is not atheism but idolatry as worship of false gods. In this sense, theologians like Paul Richard, Severino Croatto, Jorge Pixley, Franz Hinkelammert, Hugo Assmann, among others, reflected on the fetish character of the capitalist system (Vv. Aa., 1989). Therefore, they reclaimed one of the major themes in the biblical tradition, which is: the battle of the gods.[3]

According to these theologians, any system of oppression requires the creation and establishment of sacralising idols that legitimise inequality and injustice. Clearly theology – or any social theory, being inscribed in an unequal regimen will fulfil a function of legitimation or critique. Hence, theology is not only an *epistemic conceptualisation of the sacred*[4] but it is also a battlefield (Richard, 1975). Where there is an antagonistic social formation, prophetic denunciation will appear.

Paul Richard and Jorge Pixley (1989: 57–77) concur that in the process of liberation lies the difference between God and the false idols. Along these lines, we can see that the knowledge of Yahweh is linked to the sovereignty of the people; therefore, it is in the deliverance from bondage the people realise a true confession of faith. Hence, it is an idolatrous act when the people subject themselves to an oppressive authority. Needless to say, the liberation theologists maintain that sometimes such liberation is violent. This consideration should not be read as an apology for violence but as an awareness of the role of *prophetic subversive violence*[5] as *Word of God* that rebukes, critiques and denounces the structure of oppression. Regarding this, Dussel (1992: 20) states that neither the Church nor the Old or the New Testament condemn violence but actually condemn the practice of violence.

> The conditions of prophetic subversive violence are different than the doctrine of non-violence or armed violence. *Prophetic* subversive violence is 'violent' (in this it differs from non-violence) as it hits, shocks, and discomforts those living within the oppressive structure. The intention is to destroy the structure, not to eliminate the oppressor, but to humanise it. This means, for example, to reveal the sin of making weapons, the mortal mistake that lowering the international price of raw materials signifies, to denounce the 'good conscience' of those who steal millions and then return crumbs as 'aid to the Third World.'

Meanwhile, Franz Hinkelammert and Hugo Assmann, two prominent members of the Ecumenical Research Department of San José de Costa Rica, showed the relevance and potential of Marx's 'theory of fetishism'. For them, capitalism must be understood not only as a system of fetishised appearances but also as a religion of daily life.[6] Analysing the binomial economy–theology, these theologians traced the footsteps of economic discourse in order to show its impact on the social environment and its impact on the eco-system. To them, economics is a form of secular theology that has its own apostles and theologians. In that sense, through studying the main tenets of liberal economic theory and its transcendental notions (the invisible hand, overall balance, the total market), theologians reveal the hidden religious aspect in the *scientific* and *secular* discourse of the economy.

Moreover, it is interesting to note that the intent of a theology of capitalism has also been made by economists such as George Gilder (1986) and Michael Novak (1982, 2008). For these liberal economists, unlimited faith in 'individual creativity' allows for the smooth operation of the market; even its economic anthropology (*homo economicus*) is reduced to the design of an entity's preferences, bypassing the conception of a subject of needs. In fact in this entelechy, if not alienation, the conception of man's concrete life is replaced by a normative transcendental criterion.[7] Furthermore, such entelechy – criticised by Marx – omits the fact that 'man is no abstraction' inherent in each individual 'is, in reality, the set of social relations'.[8] Similarly, liberal economists distort the notion of freedom by starting with private property as their core economic paradigm, and struggle for a self-referential market where there is no room for any state intervention. Of course, government intervention is only permissible when it comes to rescuing financial capital or strengthening enforcement measures against the population.[9]

Hugo Assmann and Franz Hinkelammert (1989) interpret the capitalist economy as a process of idolatry. This economy implies dire consequences, not only for men and women but also for nature, given that its interest in profit becomes the formal criterion for success. Therefore, liberation theologists use Marx's critique of fetishism to analyse the logic of capital, that is, its death dynamics. In that sense, capitalism is anti-ecological and, therefore, anti-life.

Idolatry is conceived as manipulation of religious symbols to legitimise the fetishised power; such manipulation requires sacrifices for the consolidation of the mystique of death. False gods (those of the overall market) demand the immolation of the poor. Consequently, 'essential is the practice's own "economic religion", and their rituals and holy places must be sought in the practical fulfilment of the market economy's demand and not primarily in traditional religious temples' (Assmann and Hinkelammert, 1989: 254, original translation).

In an excellent text entitled *O capitalismo como religão: Walter Benjamin e Max Weber* (Capitalism as religion: Walter Benjamin and Max Weber), Michael Löwy (2007a: 177) notes that among the unpublished articles of Walter Benjamin (in volume VI of *Gesammelte Schriften*, edited by Rolf Tiedemann and Hermann Schweppenhäuser, published in 1985), Benjamin argued that capitalism should be seen as a religion.

Michael Löwy (2007a: 179–81) notes that while Benjamin does not cite Max Weber, still three elements emerge from the ideas and arguments of the German sociologist that contain a more critical and more radical force, not only socially or politically but also from a philosophical perspective; these are antagonistic to the Weberian thesis of secularisation: (1) Capitalism is a specifically cultic religion, perhaps the most hyped that has ever existed. Nothing has meaning, which is immediately related to the cult for it has no specific dogma or theology. Utilitarianism acquires, in this perspective, its religious colouring. (2) Capitalism is closely linked to the realisation of the cult: the cult is permanent. Capitalism is the relentless and merciless celebration of a cult. Holidays and days of celebration are far from interrupting the cult, in fact they are part of it. (3) Capitalism is probably the first example of a cult that does not atone (*entsühnenden*) but seeks to find fault.

Although Benjamin does not explain the process that allows the assimilation of capitalist economic practices as a cult, he does use some images to reveal the 'worshipping' of some objects. Löwy notes that in the book *Sens unique* (*One-way Street*, 1979) Benjamin compares 'bills and bank figures' with the 'facade of hell' (*la façade de l'enfer*). In that sense, 'desperation is the religious state of the world of capitalism' (Löwy, 2007a: 179).

Furthermore, Löwy (2007a: 189–90) argues that:

> it would be interesting to compare Benjamin's *Capitalism as a Religion* with the work of the Latin American liberation theologians that – without knowing of the 1921 extract – developed from the 1980s a radical critique of capitalism as idolatrous religion. So, according to Hugo Assmann, it is in the implicit theology of the economic paradigm and devoted practice of daily fetishism that the capitalist 'economic religion' is manifested. The explicit religious concepts found in the literature of 'market Christianity', the neoconservatives for example, only complement this. The theology of the market, from Malthus to the very last document produced by the World Bank, is fiercely sacrificial: it demands of the poor a sacrifice on the altar of economic idols. Simultaneously, analogies with and differences from Benjamin's ideas are evident.

For Michael Löwy (1998: 79), the originality of this theology, in the sense that it generated a synthesis – or dialectic, as some may think – lies in the fact that it surpasses the classical opposition between tradition and modernity. Indeed, liberation theology is a product of modernity and therefore endorses the values of the French Revolution (liberty, equality, fraternity, democracy, separation of Church and state), but shows a strong hostility towards the elements shaping industrial-bourgeois society (accumulation per se, frantic consumption, instrumental rationality, exacerbated individualism). In that sense, liberation theology recognises its modern legacy, which expands its argumentative capacity – the result of its entanglement with the social sciences – for a sly critique against the 'actually existing modernity', that is, the hegemonic modernity which reduces non-Western peoples and nature to subjects without rights.

Another characteristic feature of this theology is represented by the role of utopia, not only as criticism of the established order but also as a historical project that aims towards the creation of a classless society. It is no coincidence that Ernst Bloch's reflections are present in the work of some liberationist theologians, such as Gustavo Gutierrez and Enrique Dussel. When I asked Leonardo Boff how the mystical-ecological aspect can be recovered in contemporary social struggles, the former Franciscan replied:

> I think you have to see that behind all social movements – which seek transformation – there is a mystique, in the sense that Max Weber employs that term in his famous text 'Politics as a vocation', to refer to ideas and forces that mobilise and give meaning to individuals and groups, even when these groups are defeated; said mystique keeps them fighting, where the utopian dimension is present. Utopia belongs to reality, it is the powerful side of reality and through our historical practice we can transform it into actions, movements, revolutions and changes. It is precisely that mystique which gives meaning and power to movements; when that dimension is lost, movements become bureaucratised and politicised in the partisan sense and, consequently, lose their focus and a sense of direction. Therefore, the mystique must be thought about in sociological terms – not so much in religious terms – in line with Ernst Bloch who conceived it as something that continually moves people, the *Principle of hope*, which is not a virtue but an engine, a fundamental energy of the human being, which compels her to protest. Therefore, it provokes dreams into the realm of the possible and causes strife to occur. Utopic energy is inexhaustible – the structure of desire – it is always present.[10]

Utopia as a principle (*totum*) is present in the political and social projects of liberation theologists. Ernst Bloch roughly (*grosso modo*) divides the utopias. On the one hand, we find the group of abstract utopias, projects linked to the fascist bourgeois tendency or omitting the structure of domination and exploitation and, on the other, that of concrete utopias that struggle for the transformation of society;[11] utopias that are aimed towards the socialist or eco-socialist project.[12]

It is no accident that, in turn, referring to the process of decolonisation of the imaginary in contemporary Africa, the Cameroonian thinker and historian Achille Mbembe rescues the power of hope. For Mbembe (2010: 52) 'the poetic production of memory and the religious' is the source of the imaginary and therefore religion must not only be understood as the relationship to the divine but also as an instance of the cure (*instance de la cure*). Even when referring to the theological-political dimension in the deconstruction of 'colonial prose', this Cameroonian thinker does not scant in his reliance upon the figures of Ernst Bloch and Walter Benjamin.

Neoliberalism in Latin America

With the fall of the Berlin Wall, the disintegration of the socialist bloc, the declaration of the 'end of history' and the verbiage on the inevitable victory of the free market, some thinkers – such as Jozef Stanislaw Tischner – declared that liberation theology was mortally wounded. Such statements evidence the lack of knowledge that existed (and still exists) on this theology. Indeed, liberation theology recovered the analytic mediation of Marxism in order to understand the dynamics and functioning of capitalism. However, it was not Marxist in itself.

Interestingly, in November 1990, as part of a lecture at the University of Turin, Leonardo Boff (1993: 126) noted: 'from the beginning liberation theology never placed socialism at the centre of its practice and concerns, but it was the poor'. Therefore, the approach to the analytical mediation of Marxism had the purpose of finding an alternative to capitalism (as an historical social formation), but never with the intention of copying the false caricature presented by the Soviet regime as a 'socialist model'. Hence socialism was understood as a 'historical reference' that could not be ignored. Nevertheless, the roots of this theology were elsewhere.

To understand the 'new nuances' of liberation theology, the Belgian sociologist Francois Houtart (2005: 64) suggests analysing three factors which contributed to the reconfiguration of the Latin American region in recent decades. These phenomena are: (a) the triumph of neoliberalism as a new expression of American imperialism, (b) the emergence of a postmodern stream of thought and (c) the Vatican's systematic repression of liberation theologists.

If in the 1960s, 1970s and 1980s, liberation theology had as its socio-political framework the establishment of military dictatorships; the 1990s meant not only the 'transition' to democratic regimes but also the consolidation of the free market model in Latin America. While neoliberalism was first introduced in Latin America in Chile under the military dictatorship of Augusto Pinochet in 1973, it was during the 1990s that Latin American governments adhered to structural adjustment programmes. For James Petras and Henry Veltmeyer (2002), globalisation is the new mask that conceals the true face of our time: imperialism.

Although liberation theologists do not use imperialism as an analytic category, Luis Gerardo Díaz Núñez (2009: 67) suggests that this category allows us to observe the role of the United States in the projects of privatisation and militarisation in the region. Among the economic effects that we observe are, on the one hand, the heyday of *maquiladoras* and, on the other, increasing poverty: 227 million people living below the poverty line. Not to mention the forced migration that is caused by this new context. By the year 2010 the US authorities estimate that at least 39 million Latin American migrants will find themselves on the north side of the Rio Grande. Diaz Nuñez observed convergences that led him to encompass all the countries of Latin America as a common space where poverty, unemployment, violence and marginalisation are converted into a coin for daily use. Indeed, Latin America is not the poorest continent but it is the most polarised: only 10% of the population owns 60% of the wealth, while the poorest 10% holds only 2%.

At the political level, the 'transition to democracy' has not met expectations. For example, according to Zibechi (2008: 19) new forms of domination are being born in Latin America, masked under a progressive discourse, as bio-political domination is being implemented by the left, introducing untold levels of confusion and passing off brutal forms of domination as 'aid' to the poor. Hence, three great political and social currents born in this region make the ethical and cultural framework of the great movements: basic ecclesiastical communities linked to liberation theology; the Indigenous insurgency, carrier of a worldview that differs from the Western one; and the inspiring Guevarism of revolutionary militancy. These currents of thought and action converge, resulting in an enriching *mestizaje* – one of the hallmarks of Latin American social movements. For others, like Aguirre Rojas (2008: 49), the emergence of new rights and new lefts in Latin America has created conditions whereby traditional politics is viewed with distrust. A paradigmatic figure is Luiz lnazio 'Lula' da Silva, with his trajectory of struggle and militancy in the Workers Party, which led him to the presidency of Brazil, but whose tenure was tainted by the implementation of neoliberal public policies. Applauded by celebrating masses in 2003, he encountered a loss of credibility expressed in the resignation of Frei Betto from his cabinet.

Upon asking Frei Betto what the current challenges of Latin American thought are, he commented:

> I would say that there are many and that they are articulated. First, what do we want for the future of Latin America? This implies a re-discussion of socialism. What is socialism? After the fall of the Berlin Wall, there has been no discussion on this matter. For example, governments – such as that of Hugo Chávez – speak of a Bolivarian revolution, but no one knows exactly what that means and how one would go about building one. Another issue is the return of working with the poor, because we have neglected this aspect. There was a gentrification of the Latin American left. First, because it went down with the collapse of the Soviet Union, as it had no popular roots, it entered into an epistemological crisis from which it has not yet emerged. Some became bourgeois. The part of the movement that had an effective relationship with popular movements was saved, but many were inserted into power structures: with Lula, with Chávez, among others. So grassroots work is no longer done. For example, the Workers Party (PT) no longer has grassroots core groups as it had in the 1970s or 1980s; that is, it no longer has people going to the periphery. All work, which I call Popular Education, in line with Paulo Freire was practically abandoned. Today we have a series of crises of popular movements, as they are very disjointed, for example in their perspectives. Another issue to ponder. What does power mean? I am not referring to the power of the left but to progressive power. For example Chávez or Lula and all of those; bourgeois structures. What does this mean? Noting, that often the left in power takes the right's methods. It's happened very clearly in Brazil. The development, sustainability, ecology and the Amazon are problems that are not clear. There must be a thorough debate on these issues so perhaps your thesis will be of great help to rethink these issues. The pattern of issues has changed because reality changed. But we have not yet – as

in the 1970s or 1980s – had an organic discussion on this line of issues. There is a group here, another there, but an overall of joint reflection is lacking.[13]

Diaz Nuñez is convinced that the pontificate of John Paul II plunged the Church into 'an ecclesiastical winter'.[14] The hostility towards and distrust of liberation theology perhaps lies in how little knowledge we had about this theology because it was considered a vehicle of communist propaganda. Meanwhile Michael Löwy (2007c: 317) mentions that the end of the dictatorship in Brazil in 1985 intensified the offensive against liberation theology. It is worth recalling the 'obsequious silence' imposed by the Congregation for the Doctrine of the Faith, that same year, on Leonardo Boff. For the former Franciscan:

The theologian must be organically linked to them [to the social movements] and if it were not so, he would have to renounce being a liberation theologist. In my case, since the beginning, I started working in the garbage dump of Petropolis – over the course of 15 years – where 200 families live, garbage selecting, organising communities and awareness, among other issues, and simultaneously reflecting on the matter. Therefore, from the misery of the world one must think of the grace of the world, the process of redemption that we do not bring but that we join, so, alongside the theology we must have pedagogy. How do I make it in such a way that we are not authoritarian, paternalistic or elitist? There, Paulo Freire is fundamental for us. Additionally, he was one of the founders of liberation theology. He taught us freedom as the practice of liberation and education as the practice of freedom. Therefore, we must learn from the people, exchanging knowledge; the swap of knowledge is critical, as we come with an academic background of knowledge but learn from the people's lore – within the processes of struggle and labour. So, for me, that's the novelty of liberation theology. It is no accident that this is a scandal to the metropolitan centres of learning, where the European theologian – whether French, German or Roman – lives in the academy and discusses with colleagues. But if someone asks what's behind you? The answer is invariably: we have a library. However, if we are posed with the same question, we answer: behind us are 100,000 grassroots communities, thousands of biblical circles, many social movements behind us; there is life, not a book. This is shocking for them, as we have never been understood. We have been defamed, relativised. For them, we have no time to read. Nor have we money to buy, nor do we have much time to read but we read the book of life, the book of people who are rich, much richer than written books. Benedict XVI [then the Pope] is an enemy of the intelligence of the poor, he punished the theologians of liberation, prohibited the grand collection that was 53 volumes, which codified that thought, in order to make it more systematic and prevent this whole process. He will remain in history as an enemy of theological intelligence and an enemy of the poor and, therefore, we must denounce him because he is extremely arrogant and contemplates doing God's work by repressing us and believes himself to be doing something good for the people by silencing us.[15]

Theology of Liberation in Motion

Michael Löwy (2007c: 31) identifies two prospects for renewal within the theology of liberation. Although both are different, they are not really contradictory because these prospects do not omit the central importance of the poor in the socio-economic sense but incorporate new horizons. On one side, to extend the concept of the poor as it includes the racial dimension, gender and Marxist 'classic' themes along with the new contributions of ecology. In that sense, the figure of Leonardo Boff is the sharpest expression of said articulation. The other perspective is proposed by theologians who lead in the analysis of the field of economics, where both Hugo Asmann and Jung Mo Sung find an 'elective affinity' between Marxism and Christianity expressed in the biblical analogy of fighting idols.

For some authors, such as Díaz Nuñez (2009), the emergence of new paradigms influenced the new concerns of liberation theology. For others, like Rubén Dri (1994: 69–77), the deep crisis (including the crisis of Marxism) impacted the reconfiguration of liberationist theology. In this manner, one must not just mention the failure of the Sandinistas but also the anniversary of the fifth centenary of the discovery of America, which reverberated not only in the social context but, simultaneously, troubled the comfort into which Latin American academia had settled.

Effectively, the celebration of the 500th anniversary of the union of two cultures (European and Indigenous) was tainted by the memory and the presence of Indigenous and Black groups who did not diligently assume entelechies of a common history. The National Confederation of the Indigenous Peoples of Ecuador and the Neo-Zapatista movement in Mexico stormed the *continuum of history* – in the sense that Walter Benjamin gave the term – as a reminder that 1492 represented for them the year of the European invasion, that is, the beginning of the long 500-year night.

Gilmar Mauro, head of the Rural Landless Workers Movement (MST), recognises that in the 1990s, with the continent-wide campaign on 500 years of Indigenous, Black and popular resistance, the Latin American Coordination of Rural Organisations created a space designed for exchanges between peasant movements. After the collapse of 'Soviet socialism' they were disjointed and therefore the idea of building an autonomous movement was recovered, meaning one without an International Secretary and without a bureaucracy, but instead composed of experiences, discussions and coordinated actions.[16] In this sense, liberation theology assimilated demands and movement strategies to articulate its discursive locus.

For Francois Houtart (2005: 67), liberation theology was branded as being a White theology, male and centred on class relations. However, it is precisely the consciousness of the 500 years' resistance which began drawing attention to Indigenous theology. Its leading exponents include: Eleazar López, Clodomiro Siller, Pedro Gutiérrez, Gerardo Flores, Angel Barreno, Arturo Lona, Samuel Ruiz and Leonidas Proaño. They propose an Indigenous liberation theology, part of reality and the 'ethical-mythical nucleus' of the original peoples who have been doubly denied both by Western culture and by *mestizo*-nationalist ideology.

The liberation theology of Afro-Latin American tradition (perhaps most developed in Brazil, Cuba and Haiti) claims 'enculturation' of African cultures and the emergence of Black theology in the United States. The revaluation of Voodoo, Candomblé and Santería as worthy 'heritage' has been a key element in this trend towards a theology of liberation.

In the process of deconstructing androcentric categories, feminist theology has played a very significant role. The work of Ivone Gebara, Elsa Tamez, Maria Jose Rosario Nunes, Elizabeth Schüssler Fiorenza, Sylvia Marcos, Maria Clara Bingemer and Marcella Althaus-Reid, has helped to expose the sexist atavism of biblical hermeneutics. In this sense, feminist theology realises the double exclusion suffered by women (within the class and gender structures). Therefore feminist theology can articulate a critique not only against patriarchal hegemonic modernity but also against the 'coloniality of power'. Although the proposal of Marcella Althaus-Reid (2000: 127) deserves a particular mention, as it departs from the premise that every 'theology is contextual'; Althaus-Reid complements this with the following: 'theology is a sexual act, a sexual ideology manifested in a hallowed manner: a deified sexual orthodoxy (correct sexual dogma) and orthopraxis (correct sexual behaviour): theology is a sexual act.'

From this point, Althaus-Reid questions the 'essentialist' nature that liberation theology has hatched in the figure of the poor, that is, a desexualised poor. Althaus-Reid (2000) says, '[L]iberationists were somehow Hegelians, and right-wing Hegelians at that, seeing in the institution and structures of heterosexual, *machista*, Latin American society, the movement of a *machista* God, a god of the poor, but a *machista* one.' In other words, Althaus rebukes female and male liberation theologists for accepting and reifying through the uncritical use of patriarchal structured categories, a system of economic, political, cultural and of course erotic domination, without a minimal hit to the hard core of the grand heterosexual narrative.

Analysing exegesis that liberation theologists such as Bingemer and Guebara have made of the Virgin Mary, Althaus-Reid warns of the theoretical limits, methodological shortcomings, political dangers and sexual atavism of its Mariology; since far from presenting a liberating Mary – in the broad sense of the term – it legitimises and reinforces the image of Mary as a symbol of oppression, where disunity between soul and body strengthens gender roles and the exaltation of motherhood as a patriarchal cultural product is taken to an extreme. Thus, Althaus-Reid (2000: 75) sees Marian devotion as an ideological trap and writes:

Indecenting Mary: her virginity is the first thing that must go because poor women are seldom virgins. Theological virginity must go because it encourages hegemonic memories, false memories to be shared in the false environment of heterosexuality, while the real skeletons in the cupboard are excluded from our sharing and learning as mature people in community.

Althaus-Reid's subversive thoughts disrupt not only the field of theological markets but also heterosexual discourses based on binary discriminations. In effect, sexuality is a socio-historical construct that must be contextualised; therefore, resorting to the use of gender perspectives is indispensable. Althaus-Reid relies on the contributions of Butler, Sedgwick, Garber and Rubin, primarily to challenge biased liberationist patriarchal ideology. In that sense, Enrique Dussel's erotic project is dismissed as being not only 'idealist' but attached to the edge of the 'fetishism of the patriarchal phallus':

> Enrique Dussel, for instance, considered homosexuality and lesbianism to be the enemies of the liberation project, and as such, part of what he claims to be the autoerotic individualist project of a hegemonic Totality … Dussel's concept of Totality, as so often in liberation theology, is univocal: the oppressed–oppressor categories are subsumed into heterosexualism; good heterosexualism (reproductive) and bad ones (sodomy, for instance) … Natural and procreative were exchangeable terms for the sexual act and sodomy, mutual masturbation or other pleasures outside the limits of vaginal penetration were the basis of theological casuists, the judges' court of Christianity. But what was sinful in sodomy was not considered or at least it was far more than the sexual act relating penetrative sex between a man and another man, and was seen as a threat to the social order. (Althaus-Reid, 2000: 194–95)

Hence the 'Levinasian left' becomes an 'idealist right' when it comes to sexuality, as: 'Dussel's fear of heterosexual deconstructionism shows the cul-de-sac of Liberation Theology' (Althaus-Reid, 2000: 197).

The indecent theology that Althaus-Reid presents can be referenced by the 'women lemon vendors from Argentine', famed for not having any underwear, who sell their products on the streets of Buenos Aires. To Althaus-Reid, this represents not only the close relationship between theology and everyday life but also a specific subversion of gender and sexual codes established in Latin America from the Conquest and to the present day. Hence, the 'theology without underwear', that Althaus-Reid proposes, is trying to overcome the binary logic imposed by the patriarchal model of sexual theologies – Althaus-Reid here makes the distinction between theologies of sexuality and sexual theologies established by James Nelson (1992) – as it relates to queer theory. It endorses the dynamic and protean character and inconsistencies of sexuality and identity. In that sense, Althaus-Reid's proposal is a theological and political project based 'on the experience of transgression' (Moles, 2010: 93).

However, it is no novelty to identify the relationship between the crisis of capitalism and the crisis that traverses the Oedipus complex; or to reveal the spatiotemporal concordance between narcissism as a 'pure ego depletion' of our societies, where capitalism becomes permissive and hedonistic. Long before Žižek (2004), another Lacanian – in this case a right-winger – stressed the symbiosis between transgression and the customisation process in the reconfiguration of capitalist society (Lipovetsky, 1983). Indeed, transgression forms part of the mechanism of power but also enables 'desecration' as an act of restitution of goods and uses to humans.[17] In this regard transgression does not escape the contradictions of social reality and, therefore, should not be underestimated.

Clearly we cannot exhaust the issues addressed by Althaus-Reid, ranging from religious icons (Virgin Mary, Holy Wilgefortis or Holy Librada) to sexual readings of the Bible (the relationship between Jesus and Lazarus, the tension between Judith and Mary) passing, undoubtedly, through the implications of sadomasochism, transvestism or adultery in theological musings. In this manner Althaus-Reid uses indecent images and perverted metaphors in order to subvert the patriarchal canons of theology and their heterosexual grammar. Althaus-Reid's contribution lies particularly in having placed on the liberationists' table the role of socio-historical sexuality and its implications in building the theology that is being developed in a code of liberation.

Even after the obsequies of the theology, the liberation theologian Jung Mo Sung (2009: 289) recognised that Althaus-Reid never lost sight of the economic issue. He also emphasised that her work had contributed vigorously to outline some of the limits that liberation theology has reproduced, resulting from ideologies, in her reading of notions such as gender and sexuality. Therefore, Althaus-Reid showed that 'the way of theology is not of continuity but of non-conformity'.

For our part, we argue that, despite the theoretical weaknesses that are found in Althaus-Reid's project, it must be recognised that there is a sexist gradient prevailing in conceptions of liberationists' work, not only in the theological realm but also in the political. In that sense, 'Indecent Theology' poses two challenges: first, the articulation of sexuality and the reconfiguration of subjectivity in critical theological thought and, second, enrichment, from a libertarian perspective, using the notion of class. Following Walter Benjamin, we believe we need – perhaps now more than ever – the 'weak messianic force' of the dwarf[18] to establish the *true state of exception*, meaning, a classless society.

If our goal is to 'save the world in such a manner that even the Messiah of religious traditions would remain pale with envy' (Gandler, 2009: 75), we must note that 'Indecent Theology' highlighted key aspects that allow us to more clearly observe the male dominance that is exercised within the spaces of theological reflection. Nevertheless, progressively, the 'cutting of class' – in the Althusserian sense – is being eclipsed by a denunciation of the patriarchal system. Of course, the universal project of human emancipation should not exclude the issues of race and gender; however, we cannot reduce the social form of domination to a simple patriarchal discourse as these issues would remain at the mercy of the interests that shape the exploitation, that is, the capitalist system.

When it comes to the ecological front, it has been Leonardo Boff who represents the ultimate within the theology of liberation. For this theologian, the cry of the poor must be articulated to the cry of the Earth as the system exploits not only the least favoured but also destroys nature. Leonardo Boff's approach to 'deep ecology', but above all the rethinking of ethical-ecological and social issues within the new paradigm, has made theoretical assumptions and political projects take on another shade, while retaining the same critical and libertarian core. For Boff, it is vital to create a planetary civilisation that includes the Earth as the centre of the new bio-civilisation.

On its behalf, the theology of Earth has been taken up and developed by Marcelo Barros, José L. Poletto and Ivo Caravias in order to show that the spirituality of the Earth is an urgent issue; in the face of the genocide practised by imperialism, Christians, hunger and thirst for righteousness. Therefore, they view this reality as contrary to God's promise in the Bible. The work of the Pastoral Land Commission, in Brazil, has been instrumental in the development of this trend (Barros Souza and Caravias, 1988).

Another aspect of liberation theology is represented by intercultural and anti-religious theology, which points to a symmetrical dialogue with other religions. Parting from this, an ecumenical dialogue is necessary to create a global *ethos*, an *ethos* that will not be complicit in cultural homogenisation, or the imposition of a pattern of domination. Concerning this matter, the work of Raul Betancourt Fornet and of Enrique Dussel in his 'Ethics of liberation ...' (2013) is particularly notable.

Moving along, we would like to emphasise that while some scholars argue that such an opening of the religious phenomenon by the theology of liberation shows the updating of theology with the 'spirit of the age', others, such as Jung Mo Sung or Clodovis Boff, note that this opening is more due to a theoretical side-track than to a concurrence with modern times. When asked about one of the criticisms for which liberation theology has been rebuked, that which deals with the central role occupied by the poor (as a preferred option) and now begins to be filled with ecological, Indigenous issues, etc. and how to articulate minority issues with the 'preferential option for the poor', Jung Mo Sung commented that:

I think that the dismantling or decentralisation of the poor in liberation theology responds to those positions, but also to others. With the fall of the Berlin Wall and the collapse of the Sandinista revolution, which few people speak about but was nonetheless fundamental, it was not a matter of enlightened communism. Nicaragua was Christian. God was there. I think in the loss of confidence, Nicaragua has a very important role for theologians and activists. It generated a crisis that required a structural overhaul. That is why my thesis was an attempt to realise this review. There I maintained that the structural problem was that we had impossible expectations, and that entailed theoretical and practical problems. One suggestion was to argue that the poor were not the sole subject of the revolution but that there are also new subjects. So they took advantage of the emergence of these new subjects such as women, Blacks ... etc. There was a meeting of the Latin American Council of Churches in Quito that focused on new subjects. There they maintained that the fight is not lost because there are new subjects. There is a newly formed battalion of women, children, Blacks and Indigenous people. In the end a peasant came to us and said. 'I enjoyed it but please do not forget us, the poor farmers.' That was a *shock* because it was a way to expose a problem in theology, which refers to the fact of diverting from the main issue. We have a problem that is 'history does not walk as we wish'. Marx no longer serves me so now I use Teilhard de Chardin to ensure that Paradise will come. Whether by centring on the poor, the Church, the evolution of the universe, women, no matter, Paradise will come. That is the fundamental problem.[19]

Moreover, when speaking with one of the Brazilian sociologists who closely analysed and accompanied the origin and development of liberation theology, that is Luiz Alberto Gomez de Souza, the latter commented:

> I would only say that there are not two streams but a debate within the same sector where the importance of Jung Sung Mo – with whom I have an affinity in his latest writings – is that his economic analysis is deeper. Liberation theology had made an interpretation more linked to sociology, even I am a sociologist, or Gustavo Gutierrez who relied on social science unlike Hinkelammert or Jung Mo Sung, who have worked on the economic question. Precisely these approaches grasp the vitality of liberation theology as they show the different trends or concerns. I think Jung Mo Sung is a very careful thinker and very firm in some of his contributions. Moreover, I think we all agree that this idea of the 'abstract poor' should be concretised in the faces of the excluded, from this process arise all these variants. Perhaps some – more traditional – are left only with the category of 'poor', but today there is a tendency to see the different faces of the poor in the various forms of exclusion, and this view also includes Gaia, Planet Earth. In this regard, Leonardo Boff says that not only the poor – and excluded – but also the planet is threatened. That is why horizons have been broadened and, due to this broadening, each one gives a different contribution.[20]

To conclude, we believe that the importance, impact and relevance of liberation theology should not be measured by the sound it produces; meaning, through media coverage and advertising of Academic Showcase. It is evident that liberation theology no longer has the same intensity as before; however, it is relevant to note the Nietzschean reflection, which holds that 'true events arrive on doves' feet'. Also, Achille Mbembe (2010: 35), in his work entitled *Sortir de la grande nuit: essai sur l'Afrique décolonisée*, confesses that for a long time he tried to understand the 'meaning' of the crucifixion of Christ until one day, by chance, reading Gustavo Gutierrez' book *Théologie de la liberation*, he was able to rethink Christianity as memory and language for insubordination, as a narrative of liberation and relation to an event (événement). Liberation theology allowed this African thinker to conceive of Christianity 'or the religious' not only as a critical account of authority, as a social poetry, as a subversive dream, a partisan recall, but as a precondition to the entire historical experience of the world.

Notes

1 Civilising Paradigms and Colonial Atavisms: Power and Social Sciences

1. Here we should emphasise that for Marx (2007), the form means concrete modes of social production and reproduction. That is, it is used to distinguish specific, asymmetric and contradictory social processes of relations.
2. The logic of power and the processes of fetishisation (gnoseological, economical, historical) are intrinsically linked at the socio-political level but also in the epistemic space. It is worth stating here that for us reality is more complex than theory (Feyerabend, 1989) and, in this sense, the separation of reality at different planes is solely analytical.
3. The opposition or false antonym – to use Wallerstein – between understanding and explanation was an obstacle for theoretical-methodological development in the social sciences historically. The dichotomy between nomothetic sciences and ideographic sciences is as dangerous as that between society and the individual. There is a need for an Other thinking (Khatibi, 1983) in order to understand-explain the tensions, struggles and contradictions lurking in the socio-historical framework.
4. Walter Mignolo (2007: 35) highlighted the strong potential of *border thinking* or *border epistemology* for the creation of counterhegemonic conceptual tools that challenge the epistemic and geopolitical 'truths' of power. For Mignolo, the distinction between imperial difference and colonial difference is transcendental because it points to different moments-spaces that have been geopolitically set by the logic of capital and colonial power.
5. Capital is not only an object of analysis. It is, at the same time, a specific social relation. Just as capitalism in the centre is different from that in the periphery, the process of coloniality in Mexico is different from that of Peru or that of Argentina. Nevertheless, in both processes we can find certain similarities, such as: racism, violence, repression, ontic suppression and ontological negation.
6. The first caravels constructed by the Lusitanians in 1441 were not the most advanced in the science of navigation. The Chinese junks, for example, measured 120 metres long by 35 metres wide and could transport up to 1000 tons. Columbus' *Santa María* was 28 metres wide. Gavin Menzies (2003) and Enrique Dussel (2004) point out that by 1423 the Chinese had already mapped the globe and were conscious of the roundness of the Earth. The

importance of China as a cultural and economic power until the eighteenth century has also been documented by Kenneth Pomeranz (2004).

7.

> The voyage to the intellectual paradise of Beijing also offered foreign potentates and envoys many earthly delights. Carried in sumptuous comfort aboard the leviathan ships, they consumed the finest foods and wines, and pleasured themselves with the concubines whose only role was to please these foreign dignitaries. The formal inauguration of the Forbidden City was followed by a sumptuous banquet. Its scale and opulence emphasized China's position at the summit of the civilized world. In comparison, Europe was backward, crude and barbaric. Henry V's marriage to Catherine of Valois took place in London just three weeks after the inauguration of the Forbidden City. Twenty-six thousand guests were entertained in Beijing, where they ate a ten-course banquet served on dishes of the finest porcelain; a mere six hundred guests attended Henry's nuptials and they were served stockfish (salted cod) on rounds of stale bread that acted as plates. Catherine de Valois wore neither knickers nor stockings at her wedding; Zhu Di's favourite concubine was clad in the finest silks and her jewellery included cornelians from Persia, rubies from Sri Lanka, Indian diamonds and jade from Kotan (in Chinese Turkestan). Her perfume contained ambergris from the Pacific, myrrh from Arabia and sandalwood from the Spice Islands. China's army numbered one million men, armed with guns; Henry V could put five thousand men in the field, armed only with longbow, swords and pikes. The fleet that would carry Zhu Di's guests home numbered over a hundred ships with a complement of thirty thousand men; when Henry went to war against France in June of that year, he ferried his army across the Channel in four fishing boats, carrying a hundred men on each crossing and sailing only daylight hours. (Menzies, 2003: 63)

8. Weber (2004), Habermas (1998) and Touraine (1999), among others, argue that modernity is a phenomenon endogenous to Europe. This regional or provincial perspective undoubtedly omits diverse global factors that condition such process.

9. In the *telos* of modernity, the barbarian is guilty and should be redeemed by immaculate reason.

10. There is an interesting debate between Quijano and Mignolo concerning racial classification. While Quijano describes racism starting in the sixteenth century and treats the modern/colonial foundation of racism in terms of Whites, Indians, Blacks and *mestizos*, Mignolo maintains that the category of White did not yet exist in that century, given that 'purity of blood' was thought of in religious terms and in relation to Christianity. The conversion of blood purity from religion to the colour of one's skin occurs towards the end

of the eighteenth century and has its basis in the speculations of Arthur de Gobineau. Despite this point of contention, both are convinced that from the sixteenth century an asymmetrical classification of groups and individuals linked to the Western imaginary was in gestation.

11. Bartolomé de Las Casas estimated that between 1495 and 1503 more than 3 million people had disappeared from the Caribbean islands.

12. The question as to whether Spanish colonialism could be considered capitalist has been the subject of countless debates. One of the most interesting was held between Ernesto Laclau and André Gunder Frank, who argued over the nature of the workforce in the Spanish colonies: free or feudal? For his part, Wallerstein agrees with Laclau in that the workforce in the colonies was feudal, but insists that despite this the Spanish colonies were part of the world capitalist system (Laclau, 1969; Frank, 1969, 1972).

13. Dussel mentions that in 1504 the first slaves in Santo Domingo arrived from Spain.

> In 1520 the island of Hispaniola ended its gold cycle and began its sugar cycle. With the tropical production of sugar, cacao and tobacco, came the exploitation of the African workforce, brought to live and die at the refineries, work objectified in the original value of capital. (1994: 154)

The slave was conceived universally and objectively as merchandise, as a workforce without the prerogative of becoming *formally free*.

14.
> This structure of appropriation of workforce appears to be identified with a whole system of racial contempt: the Indians suffer the internal colonialism of Whites and Mestizos, ideologically blessed by the dominant culture, in the same way that Central American countries suffer foreign colonialism. (Galeano, 1997: 106)

15. In his *Negative dialectics*, Adorno (1990) looks at implicit commodification in alienated social relations. Identity, as the culmination of a universal project, reifies the relations of domination. The struggle between the *universal absolute* and the non-identities constitutes the grid.

16. There is a vast amount of literature on Indigenous struggles and resistance from the sixteenth century until our time. Memory, tradition and imaginaries are alive in the conflicts of today (Dussel, 1994; Galeano, 1997; Matamoros, 2005).

17. Dussel (1969) emphasises that the Semites conceive mankind as indivisible. It is a position in between the Greek anthropic dualism and the ontological hierarchic dualism or pluralism of Persian religions. The Semite would not accept the annihilation of the individual after death. Among the Israelites, Hebrew anthropology elaborated a dialectic between the flesh (*basár*) and the spirit (*rúaj*) that would permit an inalterable sense of human existence

that is expressed in the word *néfesh*. This explains why the Phoenicians did not cremate corpses but buried them in sarcophagi. A human being is identically flesh-spirit, a carnal living I, all that assumed to the name of each, which relates to their irreducible individuality. The metaphysical structures of Semite thinking, at the anthropological level, would always oppose *ensomátosis* or transmigration of the soul into different bodies. Furthermore, Dussel argues (1969: 28) that *basár* cannot be translated into body because this notion does not exist in Hebrew understanding; rather it is the flesh or the material manifestation of *néfesh*. The 'body', in the Greek or Cartesian sense of the word is nothing more than the corpse (*gufah*). The New Testament would translate *basár* by using *sárx* (flesh) and not by *sóma* (body). John the Evangelist would say: 'The Word became flesh' (John 1:14). A Greek would say 'The Word took on a body', which is radically different.

18. There has also been a theorisation of the coloniality of being, concerning the metaphysical or ontological aspects that subsume the Other to hegemonic totality. Khatibi (1983), Fanon (2004), Dussel (1985) and Mignolo (2003), among others, have recognised the taxing character of colonial thought in the heart of philosophy and social sciences.

19.

> Therefore, each form of control over work was associated with a particular race. Consequently, the control over a specific form of work could at the same time be the control over a specific dominated group of people. A new technology of domination/exploitation, in this case race/work, was articulated in the manner in which they appeared naturally associated. This, which continues today, has become exceptionally successful … the rest of all colonised regions and populations incorporated into the new world market or on their way to being colonised under European domination, basically remained under unsalaried labour relations even though, of course, that labour, resources and products were articulated in a chain of transfer of value and benefits controlled by Europe … the fact remains that, from the very beginning of America, the future Europeans associated non-wage or non-salaried labour with dominated races, because they were inferior races. (Quijano, 2000: 205–07; this is an original translation)

20.

> The Venezuelan Constitution of 1839 declares, for example, that only married men, older than 25 years of age, who are literate, proprietors and generate an income not less than 400 pesos can be considered citizens. Citizenship acquisition is, therefore, a sieve through which only persons whose profile matches the requirements of the Modernity project can pass: male, white, father, Catholic, proprietor, literate and heterosexual. The individuals who did not meet these requirements (women, servants, the mad, the illiterate, Blacks, heretics, the enslaved, Indians, homosexuals,

dissidents) would be kept out of the 'literate city', and kept in the field of illegality, submitted to punishment and therapy by the very same ones who excluded them. (Castro-Gómez, 2000: 149; this is an original translation)

21. Enrique Dussel argues that in the first Eurocentrism (Kant, Hegel, Marx, Weber) as well as in the second (Touraine, Habermas, Taylor, Adorno) the Iberian and Lusitanian worlds were excluded from the modern imaginary.

22.

> Ordinances were not written on how to be a good peasant, good Indian, Black or Gaucho, as these types of humans were seen as those belonging to the field of barbarism. Ordinances were written on how to be 'good citizens' to reform part of the *civitas*, the legal space which is inhabited by the epistemological, moral and aesthetic subjects who need modernity ... The ordinances of city-living became the new Bible, which would indicate the appropriate behaviour of such citizens in the most diverse situations of life, as the extent of his success in the *civitas* terrain and in the material kingdom of civilisation would depend on faithful obedience to such norms. The 'entrance' to the banquet of modernity required compliance with a normative prescription that would serve to distinguish the members of the new urban class that began to emerge in all of Latin America during the second half of the nineteenth century ... The 'process of civilisation' brings with it a growth of the threshold of shame, because it became necessary to clearly distinguish all those social strata that did not belong to the *civitas* ... 'Civility' and 'civic education' served, therefore, as pedagogical taxonomies which separated the coat-tails from the ponchos, proper from filth, the capital from the provinces, the republic from the colony, civilisation from barbarism ... there exists, then, a direct relation between language and citizenship, between grammar and the ordinances of civility. In these cases, it is all about making the *homo economicus*, the patriarchal subject in charge of pushing and carrying out the modernisation of the Republic. From the normativity of the word, the grammars seek to generate a culture of 'well saying' with the purpose of avoiding 'the vicious practices of popular parlance' and the gross barbarism of the plebeians. (Castro-Gómez, 2000: 149–51)

23. Castro-Gómez argues that:

> Modernity is a 'project' to the extent that its disciplinary devices are anchored in a double juridical governance. On the one hand, that which is exercised within the nation-states in its intention of creating homogeneous identities through policies of subjectivity; on the other hand, governance exercised externally by hegemonic powers of the modern/colonial world-system, in its attempt to assure the flow of raw materials from the periphery to the centre. Both processes form part of a structural dynamic. (2000: 153)

24. Wallerstein (1991) argues that the emergence of the social sciences was oriented to the legitimacy of modern nation-states. Economics (market), political science (the state) and sociology (society) acted according to the reconfiguration of the world-system in the nineteenth century. With regard to this Castro-Gómez (2000: 154) says:

> the social sciences were constituted in this space of modern/colonial power and the ideological knowledge generated by it. From this point of view, the social sciences were not conducive to an 'epistemological break' in the face of ideology; rather, the colonial imaginary impregnated its entire conceptual system from the start ... the social sciences operated structurally as an 'ideological apparatus' which, with doors towards the inside, legitimised exclusion and discipline of those who did not adjust to the profile of subjectivity and who needed the State to implement the policies of modernisation. With doors open towards the outside, in return, the social sciences legitimised the international division of labour and inequality in terms of trade and commerce between the centre and periphery. That is to say, the great social and economic benefits which European powers were obtaining from dominating its colonies.

25. Quijano and Mignolo have insisted that the coordination of formally free labour was a European prerogative, and that the coloniality of power was a racial imposition within the dynamics of incipient capitalism in the sixteenth century.

26. The first shipment of precious metals from the Antilles arrived in 1503, and the sacking of Aztec treasures began in 1519. In the Eurocentric Weberian narrative, attention is not given to that narrative in the formation of historical capitalism. For example, Jeje mine, located in Ouro Preto (Minas Gerais), like other mines throughout Brazil, Mexico and Peru, was significant for the development of European capitalism. The relation between the Baroque and the plundering of resources in Latin America should not be delinked (Neves, 1986). Without falling into vulgar economicism, we should recognise the importance of material conditions in the dynamic of cultural aesthetics of a particular kind. Enrique Dussel (2001: 425) writes about Baroque culture, which: 'became the second geo-culture of modernity. Culture of hybrids, of the exuberant, of colour, of the golden (from the precious metals of Hispanic America), the hierarchies, of the interior, of the clear-dark.'

27. England, in its process of industrialisation, had its surplus population sent to the colonies. Between 1800 and 1950, 21 million people left Great Britain for the colonies. Dussel (1994) has pointed out that the state in Europe was constituted thanks to the existence of its colonies. Hegel was conscious of the importance of the colonies for the lodging of the poor.

28. The 'first vacuum' took place when China retreated from the 'world market' in 1424. Marx (2007) argued that market expansion, as in all exchange, can

result in production growth. In this sense, by closing off its borders, China allowed for 'the rise of the West'. The 'second vacuum' was forged in the eighteenth century, when China became incapable of producing merchandise industrially, due to its agrarian crisis and lack of carbon (Dussel, 2004).

29. Boaventura de Sousa Santos (Santos, 2003) uses the concept of *epistemicide* in reference to the subalternisation of knowledge, secured in the nineteenth century by European powers: Germany, France and England.

30. Foucault (1976) conducted an excellent archaeology of the human sciences, demonstrating the continuities and discontinuities with Western *episteme*.

31. Gianni Vattimo (1998b) makes the distinction between hard truths and soft truths. For him, hard truths are products of metaphysical enlightenment projecting a single narrative, while soft truths comprise the exercise of emancipatory hermeneutics.

32. Mignolo emphasises that the emergence of a Black Creole consciousness in Haiti is different, as it was limited to French colonialism and African heritage.

33. Pierre Bourdieu distinguishes different types of capital. For us, however, we fundamentally believe in aggregating corporeal capital to designate the somatic qualities of individuals and groups. Far from taking a position similar to that of Arthur de Gobineau, we consider it necessary to factor in the importance of the body and all that it implies (somatic qualities and phenotypes) in the social relations of Latin America. Quijano's proposal is based on the idea of race, and corporeal capital is therefore the foundation of our 'coloniality of doing'.

34. Galeano (1997: 2) writes:

> Along the way we have even lost the right to call ourselves Americans, although the Haitians and the Cubans appeared in history as new people a century before the Mayflower pilgrims settled on the Plymouth coast. For the world today, America is just the United States; the region we inhabit is a sub-America, a second-class America of nebulous identity. Latin America is the region of open veins.

35. During his presidency, the US Army established its base in Guantanamo (1903), invaded Santo Domingo (1904) and occupied Cuba (1906).

36. This is a term coined by theologians of liberation in Latin America, alluding to the asymmetrical relation between the centre and the periphery of the world economic system. Jung Mo Sung (2008: 10–30) analyses this term at length in *Theology and economy*.

37. That is, disarticulated in the discursive framework, as we know that social hegemonic form overlaps all spheres of reality. In this sense, we are conscious that the political is economic and, going further, that it is cultural, religious, etc. and vice versa. To say, thus, that the economic stands alone, as Luhmann (1998) would claim, is an entelechy that legitimises the *telos* of domination.

38. Here, we use Leonardo Boff (2000: 23) to refer to the nihilist aspect of postmodernity, which, through its attempt at being irreverent to reason, falls into a relativism that is not only naïve but also perverse.

39. Together with Enrique Dussel we maintain that: 'among the violence that Vattimo (Nietzsche or Heidegger) attributes to the modern instrumental-strategic *ratio*, [is] that which was used to annihilate non-European cultures of the planet' (2002: 39).

40. We should emphasise that, for Lyotard (2005: 30), there exist many modes of destruction or de-legitimation. According to him: 'Auschwitz can be taken as a paradigmatic name', given that a people was physically destroyed. This was the intention and the crime was carried out. However, and far from circumventing the historical importance of Auschwitz, we concur with the recently departed poet of Négritude, Aimé Césaire (1994: 12) that what that bourgeois humanist of the twentieth century condemns Hitler for:

    is not crime in itself, the crime against man, it is not the humiliation of man as such, it is the crime against the white man, the humiliation of the white man, and the fact that he applied to Europe colonialist procedures which until then had been reserved exclusively for the Arabs of Algeria, the coolies of India, and the blacks of Africa.

41. See the general definitions of power and domination given by the Heidelberg philosopher (Weber, 1999: 70).

42. We refer to the *piquetero* movement in Argentina, the commune of El Alto in Bolivia, the MST in Brazil, the radical sectors of CONAI in Ecuador and the Neo-Zapatista movement in south-east Mexico.

43. In *The philosophy of liberation* (Dussel, 1985) suggests thinking about the Other from the outside in order to make the distinction between the differences within identity as Eurocentric totality.

44. For Bhahba (1995), localisation is significant in the viewing angle, as it marks the material, subjective and discursive conditions of the enunciator.

45. In contrast to those who reduce Frantz Fanon to a simple apologist of violence, we think that his contributions should be considered in the construction of a political and epistemic project that take the victims into account. It is no accident that, for Alice Cherki (2000: 288), Fanon represents a thought in motion (*une pensée en mouvement*).

46. For Žižek (2009: 121), the Haitian revolution is a significant breaking process where the 'non-party' makes its own place in the social body; however, in abandoning such inclusion it fulfilled a subaltern position within the hegemonic configuration, given that the native elite continued the reproduction of the socio-economic form. That is, it preserved the mode of production based on capitalist exploitation. After the abolition of slavery, the new government in Haiti pushed an 'agrarian militarisation' sustained by the production-exportation of sugar cane and thus 'formally free' labour was not

realised; rather, it conditioned the rise of an imminent contradiction between capital and labour. In this sense, what is essential in this Marxist analysis is the unveiling of a perverse legal-ideological matrix of liberty-equality that not only masks exploitation-domination but also precisely how the form is exercised.

47. Supporting the analytical tools of Biospace and Technoregion elaborated by Orlando Fals Borda, Oscar Useche (2008: 107) analysed the relation between development and territory, proposing a re-reading of the spatial-temporal dynamic that is currently in gestation. The logic of territorialisation/de-territorialisation, in great part a product of the form of production (export processing zones, transnational enclaves), affects the reconfiguration of public spaces. Financial power has not only transformed the relations of production but also the configuration of political relations: the consolidation of asymmetries between the nation-state, kidnapped sovereignties or, as the author also points out, suspended citizenships.

2 The Shopping Mall as the Paradigmatic Figure of Neocolonial Discourse: Racism and Power in Latin America

1. This chapter is based on a piece that won first prize in the sixth Pensar a Contracorriente International Essay competition.

2. The levels of environmental degradation, induced by capital, are more than obvious. Global warming, the greenhouse effect, the waning of the ozone layer, to name just a few, exemplify our utilitarian relation with nature. Capital is ecocide.

3. We use the term that was coined by Mahdi Elmandjra (2004) to refer to the existence of an ethical-political system which, serving structural inequalities, benefits the ruling classes. Elmandjra suggests that *humiliatocracy* has become a form of governance. The relations of power between the centre and the periphery become more and more palpable at the economic and political planes.

4. While during the nineteenth century Walter Benjamin (2002) analysed philosophical and symbolic aspects of large stores, the North American shopping mall would follow in the twentieth.

5. Franco Berardi (2003) calls happy ideology (*ideología felicista*) the capitalist discourse of neoliberal globalisation. His analysis revolves around the symbolic-discursive colonisation of cyberspace and all that it implies: cultural bombardment, bio-power, virtual alienation, etc. For Berardi, the capitalist system following its own logic and to its own benefit, creates needs by consolidating social alienation and reifying domination.

6. Although Adorno (1984) makes an acute critique of the basic assumptions of the theory of the leisure class, we reclaim Veblen's (1974: 63–64) central

thesis on the process of social differentiation linked to the habits and customs of individuals and/or societies.

7. The concept of 'field' has been harshly criticised for presenting the image of a static, bidimensional and compartmentalised reality. However, we believe that the pertinence of such a notion lies in delimiting the interests (*enjeux*) that are found in dispute. Even Enrique Dussel uses this analytical figure in his *20 theses on politics* (2007a).

8. For Lyotard (2000), postmodernity is a moment of cultural eclecticism; that is, the ground zero of contemporary culture. Lyotard maintains that the central symbols (peoples, reason, etc.) of the grand narratives were destroyed, and from there emerged new discursive objects (McDonald's) signifying the end all of the metanarratives. For his part, Enrique Dussel (2002) points out that this Eurocentric view of reality is dangerous as it omits the emancipatory role of reason and the potential for social revolution.

9. The claims of psychological and physical abuse suffered by workers have become commonplace. See 'Tehuacán: la capital de los jeans' (Ramírez Cuevas, 2001).

10. For Foucault, insanity is the first discourse to be negated by modernity. Hence, for him, 1656 is a significant date in the modern imaginary, as Paris's General Hospital was built. Craziness is excluded, separated from the hegemonic discursive narrative. However, we disagree with Foucault, as the first figure negated by modernity was the indigenous of 1492 (Dussel, 1994).

11. In chapter XII of *Capital*, entitled 'Division of labour and manufacture', Marx (2007) analyses the relation between control and discipline in the capitalist form.

12. On 12 August 1999, a group of farmers interrupted the construction of a McDonald's restaurant (Martínez Andrade, 2004) at Millau.

13. For example, the posture taken by Michael Hardt and Antonio Negri (2002) suggests this idea.

14. Private television, or cable, has gained much ground among the youth of peripheral societies. *Producto 20*, a Venezuelan magazine, conducted a survey among youth between 18 and 24 years of age, and concluded that the top nine television programmes being watched are all from cable. Sony Entertainment, MTV Music, Seinfeld and Warner Channel were the most mentioned. It is worth stating here that such programmes are produced and transmitted from the USA. In Venezuela, where the survey took place, there were 250,000 homes that received cable service by subscription and another 400,000 who received irregular service, as is the case with pirate television.

15. Fanon (1995) conducted a study on the relations that are established in a colonial setting. For him, somatic relations are determinants in the habitus of subjects and in the social symbolic configuration of groups.

16. In regard to this, Frantz Fanon (1965: 35) mentions that:

The way people clothe themselves, together with the traditions of dress and finery that custom implies, constitutes the most distinctive form of a society's uniqueness, that is to say the one that is the most immediately perceptible. Within the general pattern of a given costume, there are of course always modifications of detail, innovations which in highly developed societies are the mark of fashion.

17. A concept proposed by Haroldo de Campos (2000) in reference to a counter-hegemonic logos constructed by the victims.

3   The Portentous Eclosion of the Principle of Hope: Ernst Bloch and Liberation

1. This chapter is an edited version of the article entitled 'Consideraciones en torno al hambre y a la natura dominata', published in *Revista Herramnienta*, No. 42, XIV, October 2009: Buenos Aires.
2. This means that one out of every six inhabitants suffer from hunger. The UN Food and Agriculture Organization (FAO) reports that those with malnutrition are concentrated in developing countries. For example in Asia and the Pacific, 642 million people experience chronic hunger, 265 million in Sub-Saharan Africa and 53 million in Latin America and the Caribbean. In this way, the hegemonic project of modernity has benefited the countries of the core and condemned the periphery to unprecedented exclusion.
3. Interview with BBC-Mundo, 11 February 2009: http: //news.bbc.co.uk/hi/spanish/business/newsid_788100o/7881924.stm. Accessed August 2009.
4. Alberto Nájar, 'México: cada vez hay más pobres', in BBC-Mundo, 22 July 2009: http: //www.bbc.co.uk/mndo/economia/2009/07/090721_0154_mexico_pobrezajrg.shtml. In this same piece, CONEVAL stated that the population found in material poverty is at 47.4% of the Mexican population, or 50.6 million people.
5. Here we use the 1996 English-language version (Bloch, 1996: page number) for quotes directly from Bloch, and the 2006 Spanish-language translation (Bloch I, II and III: page number) provided by Felípe González Vicén for quotes from Introductions, Prefaces and commentaries by Francisco Serra.
6. In his *Utopies et utopistes*, Thierry Paquot (2007: 17) states: 'utopia deserves all of our attention, not only as an object of social and cultural history but as a sense of hope to re-orientate our unbalanced planet'. Unfortunately, in the text, the author omits one of the most important contributions to utopic though – *The principle of hope.*
7. Michael Löwy (1986: 103) recalls that for Paul Honigsheim, 'the Heidelberg group was characterised by its disdain for bourgeois life-style, instrumental rationalism and calculation'.

8.

> But where anxiety arises not merely in a biological sense, but in a way which is only to be found in human beings, especially in the form of an anxiety dream: then it is essentially founded on social blockages of the self-preservation drive. In fact, it is simply the *annihilated content* of the wish, *a content actually transformed into its very opposite*, which causes anxiety and ultimate despair. (Bloch, 1996: 85)

9. Bloch makes reference to the contributions of Freud, Jung, Adler and Benn in order to understand the significance of 'the lacking' in anticipatory consciousness.

10. We refer, most of all, to chapter 52, 'Self and grave-lamp or images of hope against the power of the strongest non-utopia: death', where Bloch relates nihilism to fascism. Furthermore, Bloch makes a link between Heidegger's ontology and the abstract utopias associated with the death drive.

11. In his critique of Freud, Bloch writes:

> But with the existing social conditions which may by themselves copiously stimulate fear of life and death, or even produce them, the negative content in this relation is completely omitted here, i.e. that which objectively arouses anxiety, without which anxiety could not constitute itself at all. (1996: 109)

12. Against all neo-Platonisms, of which Bloch can be accused, in chapter 11 we read: 'No drive without body behind it' (1996: 48). Spinoza's thesis on the *appetitus* of all beings to conserve themselves is explicit in chapter 13.

13. The expression 'the will to live' is one suggested by Enrique Dussel (2001) to confront the Nietzschean 'will to power'. Further below, we observe the consistency of such will and how it influences the processes of emancipation and insubordination.

14. In contrast to liberal and neoliberal economists who suppose a 'preference' as the criteria of the market, we agree with Franz Hinkelammert (2002: 322) in saying that 'need' is the only criteria that makes life possible.

15. We reclaim the notion of form in the sense that Marx (2007) used it, to name the group of expressions and concrete modes of social production and reproduction, and therefore to distinguish specific social processes of asymmetrical and contradictory relations. This does not mean, however, that we veer towards an economic reductionism. Bloch rejected all types of a-historical reductionisms (Löwy, 1986: 112).

16. In chapter 53, Bloch makes an explicit link between hope and religion, constituting the utopic sentiment (Bloch III: 35).

17. Here we make reference to the works of Michael Löwy (1998, 2009).

18. It is important to recognise here that the comments of Franz Hinkelammert (2002) and Solano Rossi (2002) are relevant in so far as they maintain that the

messianic dimension is not confined to the victims, given that capitalism also produces utopic features. Thanks to Michael Löwy (2007a: 177–89), we know that Walter Benjamin found this inference, and that in his work on Thomas Münzer, Bloch invents the term 'capitalism as religion', with reference to the social relation's Calvinistic origins.

19.   For Michèle Bertrand (1986: 194), such a distinction allows us to understand the difference between conservative faith or belief, which stays behind in the illusion of pipedream discourse, and faith as subversion that struggles for mobilisation and radical transformation of the established order.

20.   Bloch (II: 485) makes reference to the transformative potential of philosophy. It is, however, pertinent to make explicit that it cannot be divorced from social praxis, as he explains in chapter 19.

21.   Applauding Baudelaire's *Paradis artificiels*, Bloch (I: 21) relates the figure of Morpheus with the opiate effects of night dreams, while linking *Fantaso* and hash with conscious dreams.

22.   Of course, we have reservations about Bloch's critique of anarchism, given that some of his postures are unjust and at times erroneous.

23.

> But the human method of production, the metabolism with which nature occurs and is regulated in the work process, even the relations of production as base, all this, illuminatingly, itself has consciousness in it; likewise the material base in every society is again activated by the superstructure of consciousness. (Bloch, 1996: 260)

24.   It is no coincidence that Bloch (II: 208) alludes to the figure of the automaton (*perpetuum mobile*) as a *telos* of capital: cheapened production.

25.   Chapters 19, 36, 42 and 55 of *The principle of hope*.

26.   'The starry sky ultimately gives the male component to the maternal feeling in nature, it gives the component of sublimity to that peaceful character with which precisely astonishment at nature on a grand scale communicates' (Bloch, 1996: 917).

27.

> Marxism as a doctrine of warmth is thus solely related to that positive Being-in-possibility, not subject to any disenchantment, which embraces the growing realisation of the realising element, primarily in the human sphere. And which, inside this sphere, signifies the utopian Totum, in fact that freedom, that homeland of identity, in which neither man behaves towards the world, nor the world behaves towards man, as if towards a stranger. This is the doctrine of warmth in the sense of the front side, the Front of matter, hence of forward matter. (Bloch, 1996: 209)

28. For Leonardo Boff (2004), the *Principio Responsbilidad* (Responsibility) and *Principio Esperanza* (Hope) are not irreconcilable. On the contrary, their mutual complementarity is necessary.

29. Löwy (1993) insists that, in Bloch's writings, the critique of technology's devastation of nature – inspired by romantic philosophy and magic traditions of the past – proposes a new technique sustained by an alliance with nature.

30. For Michael Löwy (2005b: 38), the Anabaptist movement, the Peasant War and the millennial ideas of Thomas Münzer influenced not only the works of Bloch but also those of Engels and Mannheim.

31. In chapter 33, 'Projections of a better world', Bloch claims that the dreamer always traces a superior image of hope in order to eliminate pain. Although on some occasions this image is erroneous, it should not be circumvented, given that the desire for transformation maintains the impulse for continuing to walk the path ahead.

32. For Enrique Dussel (1992: 57), those emancipatory discourses are configured on the ethical-mythical core of religions. That is, they are images and symbols that constitute what we can call the vigilant dream of an historical group. In this sense, we can speak of an ethical-mythical core constituting the cultural base of a people.

33. For Žižek (2003: 13):

> A proper starting point would have been to ask the Schellingian question: what does the becoming-man of God in the figure of Christ, His descent from eternity to the temporal realm of our reality, mean for God Himself? What if that which appears to us, finite mortals, as God's descent toward us, is, from the standpoint of God Himself, an ascent? What if, as Schelling implied, eternity is less than temporality? What if eternity is a sterile, impotent, lifeless domain of pure potentialities, which, in order fully to actualize itself, has to pass through temporal existence? What if God's descent to man, far from being an act of grace toward humanity, is the only way for God to gain full actuality, and to liberate Himself from the suffocating constraints of Eternity? What if God actualizes Himself only through human recognition?

In another work (2001: 106–7) he states:

> Here one is tempted to repeat Adorno's well-known reversal of Croce's patronising historicist question about 'what is dead and what is alive in Hegel's dialectic' (the title of his most important work): the question to be raised today is not the historicist one of 'How does Schelling's work stand with regard to today's constellation? How are we to read it, so that it will still say something to us?', but 'How do we today stand with regard to – in the eyes of – Schelling?' Furthermore, the same reversal must be applied to the very relationship between God and man: Schelling's problem

is not 'What does God mean in our – human – eyes? Does He still mean anything? Is it possible to account for human history without any reference to God? Is God just a projection of human fantasies?', but the opposite one: 'What does man mean in the eyes of God?' That is to say: one should never forget that Schelling's starting point is always God, the Absolute itself; consequently, his problem is: 'What role does the emergence of man play in the Divine life? Why – in order to resolve what kind of deadlock – did God have to create man?' Within this context, the criticism of 'anthropo-morphism' apropos of Schelling's use of psychological observations in his description of the Divine life again misses the point: 'anthropomorphism' in the description of the Divine life is not only not to be avoided; it is, rather, to be openly endorsed – not because man is 'similar' to God, but because man directly is part of the Divine life, that is, because it is only in man, in human history, that God fully realizes Himself, that He becomes an actual Living God. (Žižek, 2001: 106–07)

34. The Glorious Thirty or *Les Trente Glorieuses* refers to the period starting in 1945 up until 1973, to refer to the countries that achieved economic expansion and maintained a low unemployment rate. The oil crisis of 1973 was, among others, one of the factors that put an end to such expansion.

35. For his part, Michael Löwy (1976: 3) mentions that, during an interview he held with Ernst Bloch in March 1974 at Tübingen, he was surprised by one of the comments that the German philosopher expressed, which summarised the dedication of an entire life to the idea of utopia:

> The world as it exists is not true. There exists a second concept of truth which is not positivistic, which is not founded on a declaration of facticity, on 'verification through the facts,' but which is instead loaded with value (*wertgeladen*) – as, for example, in the concept 'a true friend,' or in Juvenal's expression *Tempestas poetica* – that is, the kind of storm one finds in a book, a poetic storm, the kind that reality has never witnessed, a storm carried to the extreme, a radical storm and therefore a true storm, in this case in relationship to aesthetics, to poetry; in the expression 'a true friend,' in relationship to the sphere of morality. And if that doesn't correspond to the facts – and for us Marxists, facts are only reified moments of a process – in that case, too bad for the facts (*um so schlimmer für die Tatsachen*), as Hegel said in his late period. (Löwy, 1976: 2)

36. As far as pollution is concerned, the countries of the North are primarily responsible for ecological damage. According to Boff (1993: 34), for example, in one year (1985), the United States emitted 1.186 trillion tons of carbon dioxide, while the then Soviet Union emitted 985 million tons. At the same time, one can only observe the hypocrisy, given that, while these same countries do not assume responsibility in changing their model of

development, they impose norms on how nature should be treated. All of this became evident during the second World Conference on Environment and Development, which was sponsored by the United Nations in June 1992.

37. Goldmann (1976: 17) says:

> What I have called a 'world vision' is a convenient term for the whole complex of ideas, aspirations and feelings which links together the members of a social group (which, in most cases, assumes the existence of a social class) and which opposes them to members of other social groups.

38. Goldmann (1976: 17) suggests that:

> not all groups based on economic interests necessarily constitute social classes. In order for a group to become a class, its interests must be directed, in the case of a 'revolutionary' class, towards a complete transformation of social structure or, if it is a 'reactionary' class, towards maintaining the present social structure unchanged.

39. The word 'utopia' comes from the Greek *u-topos*, meaning nowhere, or place that does not yet exist. It is also understood as an aspiration towards a social order or system that does not yet exist, found in direct contradiction to the existing order (Löwy, 2008: 14).

40. For Michael Löwy (2005b: 48), of all the forms of consciousness, religion holds a privileged place in *The principle of hope* as it constitutes utopia par excellence.

41. The figure of *Poverello* is key in Boff's thinking, not only as a prophetic reference (his option for the poor) but also for its ecological meaning. He left the Franciscan order on 28 June 1992, without ever denouncing Saint Francis's holy mission.

42. In *Bautismo de sangue*, Frei Betto (1984) describes the relation between some members of the Dominican order and the guerrilla organisation Ação Libertadora Nacional led by Carlos Marighella. Frei Betto mentions the importance of the figure of Leonardo Boff in his theological and social training.

43. In an interview conducted by theologian Juan José Tamayo in 1997, Leonardo Boff stated: 'My daily life consists in giving classes on ethics, ecology, philosophy of religion, and dialogue with other religions. I continue to meet with community bases, especially in Petropolis, where various NGOs operate' (Tamayo, 1999: 104).

44. The Centre for the Defense of Human Rights (Centro de Defensa dos Direitos Humanos – CDDH) was founded in 1979. Its mission is to articulate faith and justice by supporting and advising social initiatives. The author thanks the following for their help and hospitality at CDDH: Márcia Miranda, Adriana Dutra, Maristela Barenco, Silvio Munari and Rafael Capaz.

45. In an interview, João Pedro Stedile mentions that Leonardo Boff is an important reference for the MST (Stedile, 2005: 61).

46. For Olivier Landron (2008: 57–58), Boff has expressed his hostility towards proposals of 'sustainable development' based on liberal discourses that preach continuous growth. Capitalism is seen as irreconcilable with Earth.

47. In this respect, we think that it is essential to mention the interview that was conducted on 13 November 2000 by Paulo Agostinho Nogueira Baptista (2007: 398), where Boff confesses to having read Teilhard de Chardin during his years in the seminary. While Teilhard de Chardin was censured by the Vatican, Boff, as a librarian, had access to prohibited documents. The ideas of Cristo Cósmico were well nourished during those years (Nogueira Baptista, 2007: 400). In an interview held by Tamayo (1999: 132), Boff stated that in its incipient years liberation theology did not have a clear vision about the Earth, that 'moans with birthing pains', and that, as a Franciscan, he became conscious of this at an early stage; for him it was innate.

48. Within the framework of a three-month field research stay in Brazil in 2009, the author was able to observe CDDH's work and its relation to the work of Leonardo Boff.

49.
> A drop of water does not extinguish a fire; but a million drops together form a thrombus by which fire cannot hold. This historical subject, if triumphant, will be able to make utopia a possible reality, the minimal utopias of the Brazilian people: work, eat, have access to education, health services and live together with a minimum of decency. (Boff, 2006: 55)

50. During those years, Dussel (1977), made a distinction between superstructural religion and infrastructural religion. The first refers to the religion at its ideological moment; that is, as an alienating discourse of the ruling class. The second makes reference to the critical aspect of religion, religion as praxis of liberation.

51. Dussel (1977: 61) openly repeats with Bloch that: 'Where there is hope, there is also religion.'

52. This is an original translation.

53. It may be interesting to note an observation made by Alejandro Pablo Casas Gorgal (2008), who suggests that Enrique Dussel's assimilation of Walter Benjamin's work in 'Ética para la liberación en la edad de la exclusión' ('Ethics of liberation in the age of exclusion'), leads him to use the term 'victims' as opposed to 'the poor'.

54. Frei Betto (1984: 35) reminds us that US officials in Panama offered training to Brazilian military personnel for counter-insurgency. Among those trained was a man named Carlos Lamarca, a future revolutionary who deserted from the army after the 1969 coup d'état and joined with the guerrillas. Among the trainers there were even French military personnel who fought against the

Army of National Liberation in Algeria during that country's war of liberation. In the Brazilian process of modernisation, the armed forces adopted torture as a systematic method for obtaining information.

55. Michael Löwy (1998) analysed the 'elective affinity' between Marxism and liberation theology. For him, liberation theology is the most visible expression of liberationist Christianity.

56.

Scaliger himself defined the poet as someone who does not retell what already exists like an actor, but creates and founds like another God: *Videtur poeta sane res ipsas non ut aliae artes, quasi histrio, narrare, sed velut alter deus condere.* (Bloch II, 1996: 812)

57. Cardenal (2003) was born on 20 July 1925 to a bourgeois, Catholic family. From 1944 until 1948, he studied at the National Autonomous University of Mexico, Faculty of Philosophy and Letters. Thereafter he pursued postgraduate study at Columbia University.

58. Thomas Merton was a progressive priest and author of *Action and Contemplation*. Concerned with the social situation of the oppressed, he was interested in establishing a Trappist community in Central America. He was responsible for the embodiment of the counter-power discourse within the Church. With regard to contemplation as a manifestation of resistance against bourgeois life, Bloch claims the relation between *vita activa* and *vita contemplativa*. Merton's influence is also discussed in Frei Betto's writing (1984: 111).

59. Translated by Ted Chandler; found on the internet.

60. Already in the Introduction, Cardenal (2006: 15) writes:

the utopia of back then is the utopia of today, and that which has been since the time of the prophets. Now, more than ever, there are many who have faith and hope in a better world, and it seems that those who do not have it should.

61. In chapter VI, entitled 'Tito, a paixão' in his *Batismo de sangue*, Frei Betto (1984: 225–57) addresses the torture that Frei Tito suffered. He writes: 'you shall remain, above all as an example to those who fight oppression, struggle for justice and freedom, in the difficult school of hope; it is better to die than to lose life'.

62. This is an original translation from Frei Betto (1984: 273–74).

63. 'Father, I now feel happy because I know the pleasure of death. I know, by experience, that I am capable of giving my life for the revolutionary cause. My life was given for the oppressed' (Frei Betto, 1984: 209).

64. At the end of prayer, Father Marcelo read the Gospel of the Beatitudes, the Sermon on the Mount, and his comment was about the importance of Jesus in the practice of liberation (Frei Betto, 1984: 214).

65. For more on the violence of Latin American dictatorships see: *Missing* (1982, Costa-Gravas), *La historia oficial* (1985, Luis Puenzo) and *La noche de los lápices* (1986, Hector Olivera).
66. The phrase is very evocative as, besides depicting Frei Tito's trauma by torture, it expresses the discursive construction of power.
67. We make mention that, for Bloch, the utopic function – as an anthropological and metaphysical principle of all human beings – is not exclusive to the oppressed. That is why the German philosopher distinguishes between 'abstract utopias' (which consolidate domination) and 'concrete utopias' (emancipatory, in search of a classless society).
68. Bloch concludes his work with these very words.
69. We note that Enrique Dussel (1985: 9) says something similar when talking about poverty and environmental degradation.

4   The Gun Powder of the Dwarf: Unearthly Reflections on Contemporary Political Philosophy

1. Žižek (2003: 35) cites Chesterton: 'People have fallen into the foolish habit of speaking of orthodoxy as something heavy, humdrum, and safe. There never was anything so perilous or so exciting as orthodoxy.'

5   Tendencies and Latencies of Liberation Theology in the Twenty-first Century

1. Regarding this, Ernst Bloch (1996, III: 359) suggests that:

   in religion, messianism is utopia, a utopia that requires mediation of the 'wholly other' religious content in a way that there is no danger of consecration of lords nor theocracy: such as Canaan in unexplored magnificence, such as the prodigious.

2. Enrique Dussel has explored the dynamics of this mythical-ontological-ethical core to show the tension between a hegemonic discourse of domination and counter-hegemonic discourse.
3. The concept, in sociology, of battling gods (*Kampf der Gotter*) was proposed by Max Weber in order to understand the polytheism of values that are present in social tensions and conflicts. Löwy (1998: 9) employs it precisely to understand the political and religious 'ethos' in Latin America's own Liberation Christianity.
4. This is a definition suggested by E. Dussel (1992: 42). Needless to say, this is a definition that must be qualified by Jung Mo Sung (2002: 14) for whom 'theology must be understood as a hermeneutic of history to critically explain the hopes and worldviews of theoretical and social flows.'

5. In this passage, the New Testament is quoted, Luke 16:16; Acts 2:2; 5:26, 21:35, 27:41. 'Do not suppose that I have come to bring peace to the earth. I did not come to bring peace, but a sword.'

6. Supported by the work of Arend Theodor van Leeuwen, Assmann and Hinkelammert (1989) argue that Marx's critique of fetishism allows us to make the gods who are hidden in the economic discourse visible.

7. For many years, Novak directed the Department of Theology at the American Enterprise Institute. Also, Novak was one of the founders of the Institute for Religion and Democracy.

8. Karl Marx's sixth thesis on Feuerbach (Marx, 1998).

9. Loïc Wacquant (2004) observed the decrease of the social hand of the state and the strengthening of its repression. Hence, we see a reconfiguration of a state that is less social and more criminal. See also Polish sociologist Zygmunt Bauman (2010: 78). 'This institution manages something like a ghetto without walls, a concentration camp without barbed wire ... which nonetheless has watchtowers looming everywhere' (original translation).

10. Author's interview with Leonardo Boff, 9 April 2009, Rio de Janeiro, Brazil.

11. Chapter 19 of *The principle of hope* contains a deep hermeneutic of the 'weapon of criticism', that is what Marx called the 'philosophy of action'. Bloch writes, 'the ratio grows in this stretch of praxis' (1996, I: 328).

12. By socialism we refer to the political, social and ecological project that seeks the socialisation of the means of production, which gives priority to use value over exchange value, which considers quality over quantity. For their part, Marcelo Barros and Frei Betto (2009) reflect upon the relationship between ecology and liberation theology and note the relevance of an 'eco-socialist' project.

13. Author's interview with Frei Betto, 9 March 2009, São Paulo, Brazil.

14. Díaz Núñez (2009: 117) reclaims this expression from Jesuit, Javier Jiménez Lemon, which refers to the systematic repression carried out by the Vatican against liberation theologists.

15. Author's interview with Leonardo Boff, 9 April 2009, Rio de Janeiro, Brazil.

16. Author's interview with Gilmar Mauro, 17 March 2009, São Paulo, Brazil.

17. For Agamben (2007: 32–34) subjects are the result of the relationship between living things (or substances) and devices. Today, with the development of capitalism as a process of de-subjectivation, we are witnessing a great many mechanisms that challenge, control and contaminate every moment of the life of individuals.

18. We reclaim Benjamin's concept to refer to the fact that we are – as a class for itself – the revolutionary Messiah.

19. Author's interview with Jung Mo Sung, 18 March 2009, São Paulo, Brazil.

20. Author's interview with Luiz Alberto Gomez de Souza, 15 April 2009, Rio de Janeiro, Brazil.

Bibliography

Adorno, Theodor (1984) *Crítica cultural y sociedad*. Madrid: Sarpe.

Adorno, Theodor (1990) *Dialéctica negativa*. Madrid: Taurus.

Agamben, Giorgio (2007) *Qu'est-ce qu'un dispositif* ? Paris: Payot & Rivage.

Aguirre Rojas and Carlos Antonio (2008) *L'Amérique Latine en rébellion. Mouvements antisystémiques et mort de la politique moderne*. Paris: L'Harmattan.

Althaus-Reid, Marcella (2000) *Indecent theology: theological perversions in sex, gender and politics*. London: Routledge.

Assmann, Hugo and Franz Hinkelammert (1989) *A idolatria do mercado. Ensaio sobre economia e teologia*. São Paulo: Vozes.

Assoun, Paul-Laurent (2009) *Lacan*. Paris: Presses Universitaires de France.

Barros Souza, Marcelo and José L. Caravias (1988) *Teologia da terra*. Petropolis: Vozes.

Barros, Marcelo and Frei Betto (2009) *O amor fecunda o universo. Ecologia e espiritualidade*. Rio de Janeiro: Agir Editora.

Barthes, Roland (2003) *El sistema de la moda y otros escritos*. Barcelona: Paidós.

Baudrillard, Jean (2002) *Crítica de la economía del signo*. México: Siglo XXI.

Baudrillard, Jean (2003) *El sistema de los objetos*. México: Siglo XXI.

Baudrillard, Jean (2005) *La société de consommation*. Paris: Denöel.

Bauman, Zygmunt (2010) *El tiempo apremia*. Barcelona: Arcadia.

Beaud, Michel (2000) *Histoire du capitalisme de 1500 à 2000*. Paris: Seuil.

Bellinghausen, Hermann (2006) 'Respalda el delegado Zero las luchas de los trabjadores de maquiladoras', *La Jornada* (Mexico) 14 February.

Benjamin, Walter (1969) *Illuminations*. New York: Schocken Books.

Benjamin, Walter (1979) *One-way street and other writings*. London: NLB.

Benjamin, Walter (2001) *Ensayos escogidos*. México: Coyoacán.

Benjamin, Walter (2002) *Paris, capitale du XIX siècle*. Paris: Cerf.

Bensaïd, Daniel (2009) *Marx for our times: adventures and misadventures of a critique*, trans. Gregory Elliott. London: Verso.

Berardi, Franco (2003) *La fábrica de la infelicidad*. Madrid: Traficantes de sueños.

Bertrand, Michèle (1986) 'La question de la croyance: de Marx à Ernst Bloch', in Vv. Aa., *Réification et utopie: Ernst Bloch et György Lukács, un siècle après*. Paris: Actes Sud, pp. 185–96.

Bhabha, Homi (1995) *The location of culture*. London: Routledge.

Bloch, Ernst (1996) *The principle of hope*, 3 vols, trans. Neville Plaice, Stephen Plaice and Paul Knight. Cambridge, MA: MIT Press.

Bloch, Ernst (2006) *El principio esperanza*, 3 ts, trans. Delipe González Vicén. Madrid: Trotta.

Bobbio, Norberto and Michelangelo Bovero (1994) *Sociedad y estado en la filosofía moderna*. México: FCE.

Boff, Leonardo (1972) *Jesus Cristo libertador*. Rio de Janeiro: Vozes.

Boff, Leonardo (1993) *Ecologia, mundialização, espiritualidade*. São Paulo: Ática.

Boff, Leonard (2000) *A voz do arco-íris*. Brasília: Letraviva.

Boff, Leonardo (2004a) *Ecologia: grito da terra, grito dos pobres*. Rio de Janeiro: Sextante.

Boff, Leonardo (2004b) 'Where do we find hope?' Available at: http: //www.leonardoboff.com/site-eng/vista/2004/nov19.htm (accessed November 2014).

Boff, Leonardo (2006) *Florecer en el yermo: de la crisis de civilización a una revolución radicalmente humana*. Santander: Sal Terrae.

Boff, Leonardo (2008a) *La opción-tierra: la solución para la tierra no cae del cielo*. Santander: Sal Terrae.

Boff, Leonardo (2008b) *Evangelho do Cristo Cósmico*. Rio de Janeiro: Record.

Boff, Leonardo (2009) 'A ultima trincheira: temos que mudar: economia e ecología', in José Oscar Beozzo and Cremildo José Volantin (eds) *Alternativas à crise. Por uma economia social e ecologicamente responsável*. São Paulo: Cortez, pp. 35–51.

Boff, Leonardo and Frei Betto (1999) *Mística y espiritualidad*. Madrid: Trotta.

Bourdieu, Pierre (2002a) *La distinción. Criterio y bases sociales del gusto*. México: Taurus.

Bourdieu, Pierre (2002b) *Science de la science et réflexivité*. Paris: Raisons d'agir.

Braga, Ruy and Michael Burawoy (2008) *Pour uma sociologia pública*. São Paulo: Alameda.

Calabrese, Omar (1999) *La era neobarroca*. Madrid: Cátedra.

Campos, Haroldo de (2000) *De la razón antropofágica y otros ensayos*. México: Siglo XXI.

Cardenal, Ernesto (1977) *Apocalypse and other poems*. New York: New Directions Publishing Corporation.

Cardenal, Ernesto (1980) *Antologia: 'Hora o'*. Barcelon: Laia B.

Cardenal, Ernesto (1999) *Nueva antología poética*. Mexico: Siglo XXI.

Cardenal, Ernesto (2003) *Las ínsulas extrañas. Memorias II*. México: FCE.

Cardenal, Ernesto (2006) *El evangelio en Solentiname*. Madrid: Trotta.

Cardenal, Ernesto (2009) *Pluriverse: new and selected poems*. New York: New Directions, p. 45–46

Casas Gorgal, Alejandro Pablo (2008) 'Filosofía de la Liberación y Marxismo en América Latina: apuntes en torno a los aportes de Dussel, Hinkelammert y Rebellato', in Vv. Aa. (ed.) *Pensar a contracorriente V. La Habana*: Instituto Cubano del Libro/Editorial de Ciencias Sociales, pp. 190–215.

Castro-Gómez, Santiago (2000) 'Ciencias sociales, violencia epistémica y el problema de la 'invención del otro', in Walter Mignolo (ed.) *La colonialidad del saber: eurocentrismo y ciencias sociales*. Buenos Aires: CLACSO.

Césaire, Aimé (1994) *Discours sur le colonialisme*. Paris: Présence Africaine.

Cherki, Alice (2000) *Frantz Fanon, Portrait*. Paris: Seuil.

Chesnais, François and Cladue Serfati (2003) 'Les conditions physiques de la reproduction sociale', in Jean-Marie Harribey abd Michael Löwy (eds) *Capital contra nature*. Paris: PUF, pp. 69–105.

Cockcroft, James D. (2001) *América Latina y Estados Unidos: historia y política país por país*. México: Siglo XXI.

Coronil, Fernando (2000) 'Naturaleza del poscolonialismo: del eurocentrismo al globocentrismo', in Walter Mignolo (ed.) *La colonialidad del saber, eurocentrismo y ciencias sociales*. Buenos Aires: CLACSO.

Díaz Núñez, Luis Gerardo (2009) *La teología de la liberación latinoamericana hoy*. México: CIALC-UNAM.

Dri, Rubén (1994) 'Le marxisme dans la crise épistémologique', *Actuel Marx* 16 (Paris): 69–77.

Du Bois, W.E.B. (1990) *The souls of Black folk*. New York: Vintage Books.

Dussel, Enrique (1969) *El humanismo semita*. Buenos Aires: UDEBA.

Dussel, Enrique (1977) *Religión*. México: Edicol.

Dussel, Enrique (1985) *Philosophy of liberation*, trans. Aquilina Martinez and Christine Morkovsky. New York: Orbis.

Dussel, Enrique (1992) *Historia de la Iglesia en América Latina. Medio milenio de coloniaje y liberación (1492–1992)*. Madrid: Mundo-Negro/Esquila Misional.

Dussel, Enrique (1993) *Apel, Ricoeur, Rorty y la filosofía de la liberación*. México: Universidad de Guadalajara.

Dussel, Enrique (1994) *1492. El encubrimiento del otro. Hacia el origen del 'mito de la modernidad'*. La Paz: Plural Editores.

Dussel, Enrique (2001) *Hacia una filosofía política crítica*. Bilbao: Desclée de Brouwer.

Dussel, Enrique (2002) *Posmodernidad y transmodernidad*. México: Universidad Iberoamericana/Lupus Inquisitor.

Dussel, Enrique (2004) 'Sistema-mundo y "transmodernidad"', in Vv. Aa., *Modernidades coloniales*. México: El Colegio de México.

Dussel, Enrique (2007a) *20 tesis de política*. México: Siglo XXI.

Dussel, Enrique (2007b) *Política de la liberación*. Madrid: Trotta.

Dussel, Enrique (2013) 'Ethics of liberation in the age of globalization and exclusion', trans. Eduardo Mendieta et al. In Ileana Rodriguez (ed.) *Latin America otherwise: languages, empires, nations*. Durham, NC: Duke University Press.

Elmandjra, Mahdi (2004) *Humiliation. A l'ère du méga-impérialisme*. Casa Blanca: Éditions Ennajah El Jadida.

Fanon, Frantz (1965) *A dying colonialism*, trans. Haakon Chevalier. New York: Grove Press.

Fanon, Frantz (1995) *Peau noire, masques blancs*. Paris: Seuil.

Fanon, Frantz (2004) *The wretched of the earth*, trans. Richard Philcox. New York: Grove Press.

Feyerabend, Paul (1989) *Contra el método*. Barcelona: Ariel.

Filoramo, Giovanni (1993) 'Métamorphoses d'Hermès: le sacré ésotérique d'écologie profonde', in Danièle Hervieu-Léger (ed.) *Religion et écologie*. Paris: Cerf, pp. 137–50.

Flores Magón, Ricardo (1993) *Antología*, introducción y selección de Gonzalo Aguirre Beltrán. México: UNAM.

Foucault, Michel (1976) *L'archéologie du savoir*. Paris: Gallimard.

Foucault, Michel (2005) *L'ordre du discours*. Paris: Gallimard.

Frank, André Gunder (1969) *Capitalism and underdevelopment in Latin America*. New York: Monthly Review Press.

Frank, André Gunder (1972) *Lumpenbourgeoisie: Lumpendevelopment*. New York: Monthly Review Press.

Frank, André Gunder (1979) *Acumulación dependiente y subdesarrollo*. México: Era.

Frei Betto (1984) *Batismo de sangue*. Rio de Janeiro: Civilização Brasileira.

Freire, Paulo (1973) *Pedagogía del oprimido*. México: Siglo XXI.

Furlan, Pierre (1986) 'L'espérance à l'époque de la menace totale', in Vv. Aa., *Réification et utopie : Ernst Bloch et György Lukács, un siècle après*. Paris: Actes Sud, pp. 197–207.

Galeano, Eduardo (1997) *Open veins of Latin America: five centuries of the pillage of a continent*, trans. Cedric Belfrage. London: Monthly Review Press.

Galeano, Eduardo (2009) *Mirrors: stories of almost everyone*, trans. Mark Fried. New York: Nation Books.

Gandler, Stefan (2009) *Fragmentos de Frankfurt*. México: Siglo XXI.

Gilder, George (1986) *The spirit of enterprise*. New York: Basic Books.

Glissant, Edouard (1997) *Le discours antillais*. Paris: Gallimard.

Goldmann, Lucien (1976) *The hidden god: a study of tragic vision in the Pensées of Pascal and the tragedies of Racine*, trans. Philip Thody. London: Routledge.

Gramsci, Antonio (2001) *Cuadernos de la cárcel*, vol. 6. México: Era/BUAP.

Guha, Ranajit (2005) *Selected subaltern studies*. Oxford: Oxford University Press.

Habermas, Jürgen (1998) *The Philosophical Discourse of Modernity*, trans. Frederick Lawrence. Cambridge, MA: MIT Press.

Hardt, Michael and Antonio Negri (2002) *Imperio*. Barcelona: Paidós.

Harvey, David (1998) *La condición de la posmodernidad: investigación sobre los orígenes del cambio cultural*. Buenos Aires: Amorrortu.

Hinkelammert, Franz J. (2002) *Crítica de la razón utópica*. Bilbao: Desclée de Brouwer.

Horn, Gerd-Reiner (2008) *Western European liberation theology: the first wave (1924–1959)*. New York: Oxford University Press.

Houtart, François (2005) 'La théologie de la libération en Amérique latine', *Contretemps* 12 (Paris): 64–72.

James, C.L.R. (2003) *Los jacobinos negros*. Madrid/México: Turner/FCE.

Jonas, Hans (2005) *Le principe responsabilite*. Paris: Champs/Flammarion.

Karadi, Eva (1986) 'Bloch et Lukács dans le cercle de Weber', in Vv. Aa., *Réification et utopie : Ernst Bloch et György Lukács, un siècle après*. Paris: Actes Sud, pp. 69–87.

Katzew, Ilona (2004) *La pintura de castas*. Madrid: Turner.

Khatibi, Abdelkebir (1983) *Maghreb pluriel*. Paris: Denoël.

Kimmerle, Heinz (1986) 'L'apparence dans le pré-apparaître de l'art. Le dépassement des limites humaines vers l'identité et la non-identité', in Vv. Aa., *Réification et utopie : Ernst Bloch et György Lukács, un siècle après*. Paris: Actes Sud, pp. 208–25.

Klein, Naomi (2001) *No logo. El poder de las marcas*. Barcelona: Paidós.

Lander, Edgardo (ed.) (2000) *La colonialidad del saber: eurocentrismo y ciencias sociales*. Buenos Aires: CLACSO.

Landron, Olivier (2008) *Le catholicisme vert. Histoire des relations entre l'Eglise et la nature au XXe siècle*. Paris: Cerf.

Lefebvre, Henri (1977) *Critique de la vie quotidienne*, vol. I. Paris: L'arche éditeur.

Levinas, Emmanuel (2001a) *Humanismo del otro hombre*. México: Siglo XXI.

Levinas, Emmanuel (2001b) *La huella del otro*. México: Taurus.

Lipovetsky, Gilles (1983) *L'ère du vide*. Paris: Gallimard.

Löwy, Michael (1976) 'Interview with Ernst Bloch', trans. Vicki Williams Hill. *New German Critique* 9 (autumn).

Löwy, Michael (1986) 'Le romanticisme révolutionnaire de Bloch et Lukács', in Vv. Aa., *Réification et utopie : Ernst Bloch et György Lukács, un siècle après*. Paris: Actes Sud, pp. 102–14.

Löwy, Michael (1993) 'Messianisme et nature dans la culture juive romantique: Erich Fromm et Walter Benjamin', in Danièle Hervieu-Léger (ed.) *Religion et écologie*. Paris: Cerf, pp. 127–33.

Löwy, Michael (1998) *La guerre des dieux*. Paris: Félin.

Löwy, Michael (2003) 'Progrès destructif. Marx, Engels et l'écologie'. In Jean-Marie Harribey and Michael Löwy (eds) *Capital contre nature*. Paris: PUF, pp. 11–22.

Löwy, Michael (2005a) *Ecologia e socialismo*. São Paulo: Cortez.

Löwy, Michael (2005b) 'L'athéisme religieux d'Ernst Bloch (1885–1977)', in E. Dianteill and M. Löwy (eds) *Sociologies et religion. Approches dissidentes*. Paris: PUF, pp. 37–54.

Löwy, Michael (2007a) 'O capitalismo como religião: Walter Benjamin e Max Weber', in Vv. Aa., *As Utopias de Michael Löwy: reflexões sobre um marxista insubordinado*. São Paulo: Boitempo, pp. 177–90.

Löwy, Michael (2007b) *Walter Benjamin: avertissement d'incendie*. Paris: PUF.

Löwy, Michael (2007c) 'As esquerdas na ditadura militar: o cristianismo da liberação', in Jorge Ferreira (ed.) *Revolução e democracia 1964*. Rio de Janeiro: Civilização brasileira, pp. 306–18.

Löwy, Michael (2008) *Ideologias e ciência social*. São Paulo: Cortez.

Löwy, Michael (2009) *Rédemption et utopie*. Paris: Sandre.

Luhmann, Niklas (1998) *Complejidad y modernidad. De la unidad a la diferencia*. Madrid: Trotta.

Lyotard, Jean-François (2000) *La condición posmoderna*. Madrid: Cátedra.

Lyotard, Jean-François (2005) *Le postmoderne expliqué aux enfants*. Paris: Galilée.

Marín, Sigifredo E. (2006) *Pensar desde el cuerpo*. México: CONACULTA.

Martínez Andrade, Luis. (2004) *Fenómeno underground*. Tesis para obtener el grado de Licenciatura en Sociología, BUAP, México.

Martínez Andrade, Luis. (2008) 'La reconfiguración de la colonialidad del poder y la construcción del estado-nación en América Latina', *Les Cahiers Amérique Latine Histoire et Mémoire (ALHIM)* 15 (Université Paris 8): 15–28.

Marx, Karl (1998) *The German Ideology, including Theses on Feuerbach*. Amherst, NY: Prometheus Books.

Marx, Karl (2007) *Capital. A critique of political economy*, vol. 1, trans. Samuel Moore and Edward Aveling. New York: Cosimo.

Matamoros, Fernando (2005) *Memoria y utopía en México. Imaginarios en la génesis del neozapatismo*. México: Universidad Veracruzana/Benemérita Universidad Autónoma de Puebla.

Mbembe, Achille (2010) *Sortir de la grande nuit*. Paris: La Découverte.

Menzies, Gavin (2003) *1421: the year China discovered the world*. London: Bantam Books.

Merleau-Ponty, Maurice (1998) *Phénoménologie de la perception*. Paris: Gallimard.

Mignolo, Walter (2000) 'La colonialidad a lo largo y ancho: el hemisferio occidental en el horizonte colonial de la modernidad', in Edgardo Lander (ed.) *La colonialidad del saber: eurocentrismo y ciencias sociales*. Buenos Aires: CLACSO.

Mignolo, Walter (ed.) (2001) *Capitalismo y geopolítica del conocimiento*. Buenos Aires: Ediciones del Signo.

Mignolo, Walter (2003) 'Os esplendores e as miséria da "ciência": colonialidade, geopolítica do conhecimento e pluri-versalidade epistémica', in Boaventura de Sousa Santos (ed.) *Conhecimento prudente para uma vida decente*. Porto: Afrontamento, pp. 631–71.

Mignolo, Walter (2008) *La idea de América Latina. La herida colonial y la opción decolonial*. Barcelona: Gedisa.

Moles, P. (2010) 'La teología "queer" de Althaus-Reid: el anti-mesianismo subversivo', *El Títere y el Enano* 1(1).

Münster, Arno (2007) 'Günther Anders y Ernst Bloch: ¿del malentendido a la polémica?', in Miguel Vedda (ed.) *Ernst Bloch: tendencias y latencias de un pensamiento*. Buenos Aires: Herramienta, pp. 147–67.

Münster, Arno (2010) *Principe responsabilité ou principe espérance?* Paris: Le bord de l'eau.

Negt, Oskar (2007) 'Andar erguido y la coproductividad de la naturaleza', in Miguel Vedda, (ed.) *Ernst Bloch: tendencias y latencias de un pensamiento*. Buenos Aires: Herramienta, pp. 47–54.

Nelson, James (1992) *The intimate connection: male sexuality, masculine spirituality*. London: SPCK.

Neves, Joel (1986) *Idéias filosóficas no Barroco Mineiro*. Belo Horizonte: Itatiaia Limitada-Universidade de São Paulo.

Nogueira Baptista, Paulo Agostinho (2007) *Libertação e diálogo: a articulação entre teologia da libertação e teologia do pluralismo religioso em Leonardo Boff*. Juiz de Fora-MG. Tese Doutorado – Programa de Pos-Graduação em ciência da religião, Instituto de Ciências Humanas, Universidade Federal de Juiz de Fora.

Novak, Michael (1982) *The spirit of democratic capitalism*. New York: American Enterprise Institute.

Novak, Michael (2008) *Anarchy, state, and utopia*. Oxford: Blackwell.

O'Connor, James (1998) *Natural causes. Essays in ecological Marxism*. New York: The Guilford Press.

Paquot, Thierry (2007) *Utopies et utopistes*. Paris: La Découverte.

Petras, James and Henry Veltmeyer (2002) *La face cachée de la mondialisation*. Paris: Parangon.

Pixley, Jorge. (1989) 'Dios enjuicia a los idolatras en la historia ídolos', pp. 57–77 in VVAA, *La lucha de los dioses. Los ídolos de la opresión y la búsqueda del Dios liberador*. San José de Costa Rica: Departamento Ecuménico de Investigaciones.

Pomeranz, Kenneth (2004) *La grande divergenza*. Bologna: Il Mulino.

Programa de la Naciones Unidas para el Desarrollo (PNDU) (2008) *Informe sobre desarrollo humano 2008*. Madrid: Ediciones Mundi-Prensa.

Quijano, Aníbal (1998) 'La colonialidad del poder y la experiencia cultural latino-americana', in Roberto Briceno (ed.) *Pueblo, época y desarrollo: la sociologia en América Latina*. Caracas: Nueva Sociedad.

Quijano, Aníbal (2000) 'Colonialidad del poder, eurocentrismo y América Latina', in Edgardo Lander (ed.) *La colonialidad del saber: eurocentrismo y ciencias sociales*. Buenos Aires: CLACSO.

Quijano, Aníbal (2001) 'Colonialidad del poder. Cultura y conocimiento en América Latina', in Walter Mignolo (ed.) *Capitalismo y geopolítica del conocimiento*. Buenos Aires: Ediciones del Signo.

Ramírez Cuevas, J. (2001) 'Tehuacán: la capital de los jeans', in *Masiosare dominical*, supplement of *La Jornada* (Mexico) 29 June.

Richard, Pablo (1975) *Cristianismo, lucha ideológica y nacionalidad socialista*. Salamanca Sígueme.

Ritzer, George (1999) *La McDonalización de la sociedad*. Barcelona: Ariel.

Rosenzweig, Franz (2003) *L'étoile de la rédemption*. Paris: Seuil.

Rossi, Luiz Alexandre S. (2002) *Messianismo e modernidade*. São Paulo: Paulus.

Santos, Boaventura de Sousa (2002) *Um discurso sobre as ciências*. Porto: Afrontamento.

Santos, Boaventura de Sousa (ed.) (2003) *Conhecimento prudente para uma vida decente*. Porto: Afrontamento.

Stedile, João Pedro and Bernardo Mançano (2005) *Brava gente*. São Paulo: Fundação Perseu Abramo.

Sung, Jung Mo (2002) *Sujeito e sociedades complexas*. Rio de Janeiro: Vozes.

Sung, Jung Mo. (2008) *Teologia e economia. Repensando a teologia da libertação e utopias*. São Paulo: Fonte Editorial.

Sung, Jung Mo (2009) 'Teologia indecente em luto', *Estudos de Religião* 23 (36, Jan.–June).

Tamayo, Juan José (1999) *Leonardo Boff: ecología, mística y liberación*. Bilbao: Desclée de Brouwer.

Tocqueville, Alexis de (2000) *Democracy in America*, trans. George Lawrence. New York: Harper Perennial Modern Classics.

Touraine, Alain (1999) *Crítica de la modernidad*. Buenos Aires: FCE.

United Nations (2009) *The Millennium Development Goals Report*. New York: United Nations.

Useche, Oscar (2008) *Los nuevos sentidos del desarrollo. Ciudadanías Emergentes, Paz y Reconstitución de lo Común*. Bogotá: UNIMINUTO.

Vattimo, Gianni (1998a) *La sociedad transparente*. Barcelona: Paidós.

Vattimo, Gianni (1998b) *El fin de la modernidad. Nihilismo y hermenéutica en la cultura posmoderna*. Barcelona: Gedisa.

Veblen, Thorstein (1974) *Teoría de la clase ociosa*. México: FCE.

Vedda, Miguel (2007) 'Tragedia, actualidad, utopía. A propósito de las controversias entre el joven Lukács y el joven Bloch', in Miguel Vedda (ed.) *Ernst Bloch: tendencias y latencias de un pensamiento*. Buenos Aires: Herramienta, pp. 97–110.

Vv. Aa. (1989) *La lucha de los dioses. Los ídolos de la opresión y la búsqueda del Dios liberador*. San José de Costa Rica: Departamento Ecuménico de Investigaciones.

Wacquant, Loïc (2004) *Punir les pauvres*. Paris: Agone.

Wallerstein, Immanuel (1991) *Unthinking social science*. Cambridge: Polity Press.

Wallerstein, Immanuel (1998) *El legado de la sociología, la promesa de la ciencia social*. Caracas: Nueva Sociedad.

Wallerstein, Immanuel (1999) *Después del liberalismo*. México: Siglo XXI.

Weber, Max (1999) *Economía y sociedad*. México: FCE.

Weber, Max (2004) *La ética protestante y el espíritu del capitalismo*. México: Colofón.

Weber, Max (2004 [1919]) *The vocation lectures*. Indianapolis, IN: Hackett.

Zibechi, Raúl (2008) *Autonomías y emancipaciones: América latina en movimiento*. México: Bajo Tierra-Sísifo Ediciones.

Žižek, Slavoj (2001) *The fragile absolute or, Why is the Christian legacy worth fighting for?* London: Verso.

Žižek, Slavoj (2003) *The puppet and the dwarf: the perverse core of Christianity*. Cambridge, MA: Cambridge.

Žižek, Slavoj (2004) *La subjectivité à venir: essais critiques sur la voix obscène*. Paris: Climats.

Žižek, Slavoj (2006) 'The liberal Communists of Porto Davos', *In these times*, 11 April, http://inthesetimes.com/article/2574.

Žižek, Slavoj (2007) *En defensa de la intolerancia*. Madrid: Sequitur.

Žižek, Slavoj (2009) *First as tragedy, then as farce*. London: Verso.

Index

Compiled by Sue Carlton

Page numbers followed by n refer to the notes

coloniality of power 3, 7–13, 22, 24, 36, 44, 115, 126n
colonisation 6, 21, 47, 52, 94
Columbus, Christopher 5
commercialisation 35, 37
communism 91, 100, 119
Comte, Auguste 18
concrete abstraction 62, 68
concrete technique 64, 68–9
conflict
    permanent 30–1
        see also Latin America and Caribbean, struggles for liberation; struggles and resistance
consensus populi 27, 94
consumption 38, 39–40, 52, 100
    and the body 42–3
    merchandise 42, 52
    and social difference 39–40, 42, 43
Cordero, Ernesto 59
Coronil, Fernando 51
corporeality 48–50, 51, 61
    corporeal capital 50, 51
    hegemonic 48–9, 50
    and social relations 48–50
criollos 10, 12, 13, 21, 22, 31, 53
crisis, and transition 81
Critical Theory 93
Croatto, Severino 104
Cuban revolution (1959) 103
Cur Deus Homo (St Anselmo) 70

de-fetishisation 20, 31, 37, 104
de-indigenisation 23
decolonisation 20–3, 27, 31–6, 94
    failure of 31–2
    of the imaginary 109
deforestation 16, 59, 76
democracy 64, 72, 76, 78, 84, 96–7
    direct 35
    particpatory 29, 99
    representative 54
    transition to 110

dependency theory 7, 20, 25, 104
Descartes, René 6, 48, 95, 97
destiny 70
Díaz Núñez, Luis Gerardo 71, 110, 112, 113, 140n
dictatorships 28, 52, 64, 71, 82, 110, 112
Dilthey, Wilhelm 73
discipline 11, 22, 126n, 130n
    and power 45–6
discursive practices 9, 11, 12, 21, 37, 40, 41–2, 46, 52–4
domination 3, 7–9, 12–13, 20, 40–1, 46–7, 101, 124n, 129n
    and concept of habitus 11
    and hegemonic discourse 54, 55
    and internal coloniality 53
    legitimate 27
    new forms of 25, 110–11
    in perpetual transformation 12, 23, 36
    resistance to 31
    role of religion and church 70, 79, 94, 98
    symbolic 42
    see also discipline; ego conquiro; oppression; patriarchal system; power
double consciousness 9, 10–11, 21–2, 53
dreams, night and conscious 61, 62–3, 133n
Dri, Rubén 113
drives 61–2, 63, 132n
Du Bois W.E.B. 10, 53
Durkheim, Emile 18, 30
Dussel, Enrique 55, 68, 89–91, 121n
    and class 26–7
    on corporeality 48, 90–1
    and discovery of America 5, 6
    erotic project 116
    and Eurocentrism 13–14, 15–16
    influence of Bloch 71, 108
    liberation 60, 78, 100–1, 118

G8 countries 55
Gaia 67, 75, 120
Galeano, Eduardo 15, 33–4, 54, 123n, 127n
García Moreno, Gabriel 23
Gast, John 24
Gebara, Ivone 114, 115
Gilder, George 105–6
Glissant, Eduard 10
globalisation 32, 35, 37, 39, 51, 110
Goldmann, Lucien 73, 136n
Gomez de Souza, Luiz Alberto 120
Gospel of Mark 94, 98
government 97–8
Gramsci, Antonio 26, 78, 98
Guevara, Che 99
Guha, Ranajit 28
Gutiérrez, Gustavo 71, 108, 120
Gutiérrez, Pedro 114

Habermas, Jürgen 13, 122n
habitus 9, 11, 38, 41, 50, 53, 55, 130n
Hammer, Heinrich 5
happiness 42, 100
Harvey, David 46
Hegel, G.W.F. 18–19, 70, 126n, 135n
Heidelberg circle 60–1, 131n
Hinkelammert, Franz 105, 106, 120, 132n, 140n
historical materialism 89, 102
Hobbes, Thomas 19
Honigsheim, Paul 60
hope 60, 77, 88, 109
    and anguish 61
    images of 62, 67, 70, 86, 109, 132n, 134n
    Principle of Hope 72, 75, 79
    and religion 62, 70, 77, 132n, 137n
    theology of 71, 93
    see also Bloch, Ernst, The principle of hope
Horn, Gerd-Rainer 91
Houtart, François 109–10, 114

hunger 59–60, 62, 82, 88, 131n

imperialism 35, 110, 118
indecent theology 116, 117, 118
independence 12, 21–2, 27, 31
Indigenous insurgency 110
    see also Zapatista Army of National Liberation
Indigenous people see Black and Indigenous people
Indigenous Rights and Culture Law (2001) 33
Industrial Revolution (Britain) 6, 16–17, 65
intercultural theology 118
internal colonialism/coloniality 13, 31–2, 53, 123n
International Monetary Fund 24, 28, 32, 54–5, 59

James, C.L.R. 31
James, Fredric 92
Jefferson, Thomas 21
Jews, expulsion from Spain (1492) 4
Job, 92
John Paul II, Pope 35, 112
John XXIII, Pope 103
Jonas, Hans 64, 68, 75
Juárez, Benito 23

Kant, Immanuel 18–19, 48
Karadi, Eva 60
Katzew, Ilona 9
Khatibi, Abdelkebir 19–20
Kimmerle, Heinz 63
Klein, Naomi 43, 52
Kondratieff phase B 71

Lacan, Jacques 81, 90, 100
ladino 21
Lander, Edgardo 9
Landless Workers' Movement (MST) (Brazil) 20, 32, 33–5, 74, 76, 114
Las Casas, Bartolomé de 94, 123n